Philosophy Mat

Philosophy Matters

An Introduction to Philosophy

Roger Trigg

First published 2002

2 4 6 8 10 9 7 5 3 1

Blackwell Publishers Inc
350 Main Street
Malden, Massachusetts 02148
USA

Blackwell Publishers Ltd
108 Cowley Road
Oxford OX4 1 JF
UK

Library of Congress Cataloging-in-Publication Data has been applied for.

ISBN 0–631–22545–5 (hardback); ISBN 0–631–22546–3 (paperback)

British Library Cataloguing in Publication Data

A CIP catalogue record for this book is available from the British Library.

Typeset in 10.5 on 12 pt Bembo
by Ace Filmsetting Ltd, Frome, Somerset

This book is printed on acid-free paper.

Contents

Preface

Philosophy is a way of thinking, not a body of facts to be learnt. Indeed it can call into question what we may assume to be firmly established facts. Yet the purpose is not to destroy our confidence in our beliefs, but to question our reasons for holding them. Philosophy encourages critical inquiry. This may sometimes be of a sceptical kind, but we may also obtain through it a renewed confidence in what we already think.

The only real way to learn philosophy is to get involved with it. No one should be content with simply finding out what others think. We should all be prepared to think things out for ourselves in a disciplined way. This is true in ordinary life in many areas, but is even more crucial in philosophical argument. This book has been written to stimulate thought and argument, not to present a bland survey of possible positions. For this reason, I have not been afraid to take up a definite stance on some basic philosophical questions, and do not always take the most fashionable view. The reader should not, however, be afraid to stop and question the argument. Anyone who reads this book, and merely accepts its reasoning in an unthinking way, has not become involved in genuine philosophy. Ideas challenge people. If a reader disagrees strongly with parts of this book, and even thinks 'that just cannot be right', the book has begun to do its job.

We should always be cautious about taking what others say on trust. This is not to say that truth does not matter, and that we can rely on our own opinions. Indeed philosophy matters precisely because at the most fundamental level possible, it is engaged in the search for truth. Nevertheless, as philosophers have always made clear, the search for truth involves using one's reason. Thinking out arguments for yourself is part of that process.

Anyone, who on reading this book, is encouraged to do that, is thereby taking the first faltering steps on the philosophical journey.

No book can cover the whole of philosophy in a short span, and I have chosen to concentrate on the problem of the nature of the world, and how we obtain knowledge of it, particularly through science. What, for instance, are the philosophical presuppositions of modern science itself? As a result, many important issues are barely mentioned. Two central themes throughout the history of philosophy have been the nature of reality and the question of human nature. I am here primarily concerned with the first, but the second is of crucial importance for morality and politics. Anyone who is encouraged to read more widely about philosophical matters, and wishes to know what the main doctrines of human nature have been in Western philosophical thought, may read my book on *Ideas of Human Nature*, a survey of twelve major thinkers from Plato to Wittgenstein. (Blackwell Publishers, 1999).

This book is the result of decades of philosophical conversation with too many people to mention. I am grateful to my own institution, the University of Warwick, for granting study leave to write it. My largest debt, however, is owed to my wife, Julia, and my daughter, Alison. Without their continuous help, encouragement, and friendly discussion, I would never even have thought of beginning it.

Roger Trigg
Stratford-upon-Avon

1

What is Philosophy?

The Origins of Philosophy

Why does philosophy matter? To answer this question we must face the issue of what philosophy is anyway. It is of little help to be told that this is itself a characteristically philosophical question. Yet the questing for the presuppositions and the assumptions which give sense to what we do is a typical job for the philosopher. Some may cynically say that philosophy is just making simple things seem difficult. It is, some may sneer, taking something straightforward and pretending that it is more complex than we thought. It is quibbling about the meanings of words. There is some truth in all this, in that philosophy must refuse to take anything at face value, in an unexamined way. A philosophy that stays at the level of common sense is not worthy of the name, not least because what we all take for granted now may often be the outcome of the philosophical arguments of previous generations. Philosophy must always encourage us to stand back from our beliefs, and look at how well-founded they may be. It involves each of us being willing to distance ourselves from our opinions, and to realize that just because we hold them does not make them true. They may well be, but we cannot take that for granted without being willing to subject them to rational scrutiny.

This idea of philosophy is as old as Western civilization. It may have little to do with being 'philosophical' about one's pain or misfortune. It certainly does not provide a philosophy of life which can help to make sense of one's existence, or give purpose to one's activities. That, some might argue, is the province of religion, if of anything. The idea of philosophy as rational questioning is derived above all from Socrates in the Athens of the fifth century

BC. He irritated those with whom he entered into dialogue (and dialogue was his preferred way of doing philosophy). His activities were compared to those of a sting-ray fish, in the numbing way that he exposed the fact that they often took for granted the very point at issue. He numbed those he talked to, because his object was, at least in the first instance, to show that they did not know what they thought they did. His ultimate aim was to obtain knowledge, but his technique aroused hostility, because he attacked people's complacency. Indeed, he became so unpopular that he was eventually put to death by his fellow citizens in the Athenian democracy. Philosophy can certainly often seem negative, and even destructive. It challenges, and makes people realize that what they take for granted is not necessarily true. Yet this can also be a very constructive exercise. It is much better to have beliefs that can be rationally defended. It is important to know why you and others should hold them. Otherwise, when eventually you are challenged, your trust in your beliefs can be shaken merely because you have not got the means to defend yourself.

It was once said that all philosophy is a series of footnotes to Plato. This is an exaggeration, but there is a grain of truth in it. Plato was Socrates' pupil, and it is only through his work that we know of Socrates' method of doing philosophy. He was also Aristotle's teacher, and a major influence on later Christian theology. The Greek world of the time was also open to influences from the East as well as being the major formative influence on later Western thought. With Plato, Eastern mysticism and Western analytic thought combine in a potent mixture. Many of the most basic themes in contemporary philosophy were first explicitly taken up in Athens. Two in particular exercised Plato. These were relativism and materialism. The first was concerned with the nature of truth, and whether there could be different 'truths', depending on who believed them. Is truth the same for everyone, even when people do not believe it? Materialism, on the other hand, was, and is, concerned with the ultimate make-up of the world. Is it only material?

The impetus to relativism came from the simple fact that the Greeks of Plato's time were only too well aware of the vast differences of belief that existed even in their part of the world. There were not just many city-states in Greece, each with their own laws and customs. Greeks were coming more and more into contact with such countries as Persia and Egypt, and their customs seemed even more alien. This process was to culminate in the conquests of Aristotle's pupil, Alexander the Great, who played a major role (in the fourth century BC) in the spreading of Greek culture and the Greek language throughout the Eastern Mediterranean and beyond, as far as India.

This ferment led to the questioning by Greeks, and Athenians in particular, of the validity of local customs and beliefs. Protagoras, for example, provoked Socrates and Plato with his talk of a true belief being only true for those holding it. You can be confident enough of the rightness of your opinions when they are never challenged and when everyone around you believes the same. When, however, you discover that not just individuals, but even whole nations, think and behave very differently, you do not need to be a profound thinker to wonder who is right, or indeed whether there is such a thing as being right or believing the truth. Do any of us believe anything because it is true? Do we even have knowledge of truth? Or does something merely appear true as a result of believing it? Might things then be true for some people or nations, but not perhaps for others?

The Contemporary Situation

Although the present world seems very different from that of Plato, we confront exactly the same issues. Our horizons are wider than the Eastern Mediterranean, but the problems remain the same. In a very settled society, perhaps of a hierarchical nature, people could accept that the way things were organized were the way they had to be. The beliefs people had, say about religion, were the ones everyone had. They seemed a part of the natural order of things. A quiet English village, a hundred years ago, would be unlikely to have people of different races and creeds walking down the street. Now, however, all that has changed. Air travel has made contact between continents easier, and there has been a huge growth in contacts between people of different backgrounds. Television and the Internet make instant communication right across the world a matter of everyday life. No one can be unaware of the vast variety of beliefs and customs and we often have to live and deal with people who make very different assumptions from ourselves. There is the same kind of ferment across the populations of the world that was once reserved for the male citizens of the Athenian democracy. How can one decide who is right and who is wrong, what is true and what is false? Do we have to? Does any of it matter? Can I just cling to what I was brought up to believe, regardless of what others think?

This last question contains within it the seeds of trouble. First, I must recognize that if I had been brought up in a very different society, my beliefs would have been different. The content of belief seems a very chance affair, depending on all kinds of external influences. Am I to say that the only reason for my holding a belief is that I hold it? Should I then go on holding it? Should I pass on to my children my set of pre-packaged prejudices, if that is all they appear to be? Is there firmer ground on which I can stand, and, better still, can I appeal to any standards that everyone ought to accept? We get drawn to the heart of philosophy with these questions. Just what is the difference between the opinions I happen to hold at the moment, and real knowledge? Is knowledge even possible? What do we mean by 'knowledge' anyway? One important factor will be that my opinion is merely mine, and yours may be completely different. A claim to knowledge, on the other hand, is not just a report about myself and my attitudes. It is a claim about what is the case. Actual knowledge, whatever else it may be, must include not just a tentative claim to truth, but a claim that is itself correct and ought to be accepted by everyone. Knowledge is of truth, and unless we revert to Protagoras' confused talk of 'truth for me' or the more general 'truth for our society', truth has a universal claim. What is true for me has to be true for you, if it is really true. What is true for you should be accepted by me as well. I cannot myself know that it is raining if you go outside and discover that it is not.

Plato came to similar conclusions, and wished to stress the importance of objective truth, namely what is true independently of the fact that particular people happen to believe it. Yet in doing so he illustrated an important part of Socrates' philosophical method. In discussing the nature of knowledge, or virtue, or whatever else might be considered important, it is crucial to know what we are talking about. Clarity of thought, and precision of language, are philosophical virtues. Socrates, therefore, was prone to ask those with whom he was in dialogue what knowledge, for example, actually is. The answer he gets in conversation with Theaetetus is typical. Theaetetus, a bright young Athenian, confidently gives Socrates a series of examples of what one can know. He talks of geometry and other things one can learn. He even refers to crafts such as cobbling. Socrates' response is also typical. With his characteristic irony, he responds that Theaetetus is very generous, because when asked for one simple thing, he has given a whole list. The point is that all of the things he mentions may be instances of knowledge, but they take us no nearer to understanding what knowledge itself is, or how it differs from true belief.

A caricature of a philosopher in an argument used to be of someone who prefaces every remark by saying that it all depends what you mean by a particular word. Indeed, in the middle years of the twentieth century, a whole industry of something called 'linguistic philosophy' sprang up in Oxford and elsewhere. It stressed the importance of clarity in the use of words, but often went further and suggested that the whole purpose of language was to analyse and clarify how language is used. It helped to spawn the science of linguistics, but it ran the risk itself of mistaking an important element of philosophical method for its prime purpose.

Such philosophy was often accused of sterility. For instance, an important moral issue is whether it could ever be justified to punish innocent people. Can one frame someone for the greater good? Terrorists might be deterred if someone appeared to have been captured for committing an atrocity. Some linguistic philosophers were tempted to duck this crucial question by saying that since the word 'punishment' implies guilt, one cannot by definition punish an innocent person. It would have to be given a term of its own, such as 'social hygiene'. This may have had the virtue of clarifying the normal use of the term, but it signally failed to get to the heart of the issue. The root question is not so much how we should describe our actions but what we should do in particular situations.

Words are tools, and we must keep our tools sharp, but philosophy is in the business of using tools and not just admiring them. Arguments about the meanings of words, or the analysis of concepts (the way we think), help us to understand what we are talking about, and what is at stake. It must however be a preparation for something far more serious. In the case of Socrates, his purpose was to clear away false assumptions before building up an understanding of what knowledge is, so that it can be acquired. Indeed Plato's ultimate aim was political and moral. He wanted cities to be ruled by philosophers who possessed the knowledge that could be used for the benefit of everyone. He did not want political authority to be the exercise of arbitrary power, as when the people of the Athenian democracy were led by unscrupulous demagogues. The latter cared more about their own position and influence than the content of their advice. Yet for a state to be governed by people with knowledge, it had to be agreed what knowledge was and how it could be learnt. Similarly, in the field of morality, Plato was adamant that the threat of Protagoras' relativism had to be faced. He had to show where moral truth lay and how it could be discovered. All this can lead to the charge of elitism, and indeed Plato's views were much admired in Victorian England, when it was believed that an educated elite had to be trained for the benefit of everyone. Yet if one believes that truth, in whatever area, is accessible to everyone, the charge of elitism can be irrelevant. The question of truth, and that of whether only a minority can acquire it, are quite different from each other.

There are clear resonances between these problems and those of the beginning of the twenty-first century. Politicians are not often thought repositories of wisdom, and can be sometimes cynically assumed to be more concerned for their own interests than those of the country they are supposed to serve. Talk of truth in morality is likely to be scorned. All too often, it is assumed that morality is a matter of taste. Very significantly, anyone who makes a claim about what is morally right will be told 'that is just your opinion'. Truth does not seem to be at stake, even though opinions themselves can be true or false. Opinions are important, but they are not enough. The difference between them and knowledge lay at the heart of what Plato was talking about. He produced examples of how, even when we were right by chance in our opinions, it was not the same thing as knowledge. A jury might be convinced by a powerful speech from a lawyer, and correctly judge the innocence of the defendant. Yet if the same lawyer had been on the opposite side, the jury would have found the person guilty. As Plato says, the jurymen (and they were men in Athens) were not in the position of an eyewitness of the crime who knew for certain what had happened. Even a true opinion, arrived at by accident, does not add up to knowledge, which is tied down in a more secure fashion.

Knowledge and Reason

What then is knowledge, and what can we know? This traditional question in philosophy is as live and important today as it was nearly two-and-a-half millennia ago. We shall not be looking specifically at truth in morality or politics in this book. Just, however, as many of Plato's writings ranged far away from those areas but were always haunted by them, even today questions of knowledge and truth, understanding and reality, have important practical applications, even though the latter are not always at the forefront of the argument. Plato was concerned with the nature of reality and our place in it, but however abstract his discussion sometimes became, he never lost sight of his overall purpose of establishing objective standards in morality, and of guiding those who were to be involved in political life. It is the same today. Discussions about the nature of reality and how far it can be known are undoubtedly essential for anyone who wishes to claim that moral matters are somehow connected with reality. We have to know what is meant by knowledge and whether it is possible before we can become clearer about the possible nature of moral knowledge. A general scepticism about the possibility of knowledge or truth will have a knock-on effect upon our understanding of morality. A general commitment to relativism in all areas will make moral relativism inescapable.

The term 'knowledge' is itself a very slippery one, and Socrates' question about its nature is still relevant in our day. Philosophical theorizing about knowledge is called 'epistemology', after the Greek word for knowledge, 'episteme'. When we turn to other languages' terms for knowledge, it becomes very apparent that things are far from clear cut. The Latin word for knowledge, 'scientia', points forward to the English word 'science', which has a much narrower meaning. It refers to a particular kind of knowledge, and not knowledge as a whole. The French 'la science' and the German 'Wissenschaft' both conveniently cloak the difference between general knowledge and the more rigorous empirical methods of the physical sciences. For example, history would be naturally classified as a science, along with physics and chemistry, by many languages, but it is not so regarded in English. One of the crucial problems that has risen since the development of modern science from the time of Isaac Newton in the seventeenth century is connected with this point. Should knowledge be restricted to the results obtained by empirical observation and experiment, along with the theories that arise from them? It is highly controversial to say that science is the only source of our knowledge. What can be known, and hence is real, has then to be confined to what is within the reach of practising scientists.

Plato himself would have found this a familiar problem. He always wrote his philosophy in the form of dialogues, following the techniques and example of Socrates. It was natural for him to begin with issues that Socrates had clearly discussed, and to make Socrates the hero of the discussion. As time went on he introduced more of his own theories, and in his later dialogues he gave up using Socrates even as a mouthpiece. In one of these dialogues, the *Sophist*, Plato explicitly faced the problem of how to define reality. In what he termed a battle of the giants he sketched the fierce dispute that he said was raging between materialists and their opponents. He said the materialists tried to drag everything down to earth 'out of heaven and the unseen'. They defined reality in terms of body and were contemptuous of anyone who claimed that something without a body could be real. Needless to say, Plato was not in the materialist camp. He believed that the visible world was but a pale reflection of a greater reality. The latter was the source of objective standards of goodness, virtue and justice, as well as standards of other kinds of perfection such as mathematical ones. He was reacting to the origins of a philosophy based wholly on science. It had arisen in the Greek world just before the time of Socrates. Its origins lay with Thales, the first philosopher, who said that everything was composed of water. It soon became more sophisticated and acquired a modern flavour with the atomists, who wanted to say that reality was composed solely of atoms, indivisible pieces of matter which were arranged in different ways to produce different kinds of objects. Even mind was to be explained in this way, much to Socrates' horror.

Plato showed himself to be a consistent philosopher. Although he is widely known for his opposition to materialism, and in particular for his doctrine of immaterial 'Forms' as objective standards, that did not stop him questioning even this doctrine in several of his later dialogues. Just as philosophy must always ask questions, the answers it gives must always be open to re-examination. There is no shame in philosophers changing their minds, and some of the greatest, Plato among them, have developed, refined and even changed their ideas over the years. Reason is never static. Otherwise it can lapse into the mere exercise of authority and the forging of tradition. Philosophy is not necessarily subversive of either, but it cannot accept them at face value. That is why forming philosophical schools and becoming admiring disciples of a great thinker, whilst understandable, can be very dangerous. An appeal to reason cannot be reduced to an appeal to the authority of an individual, any more than it should rely on the power of an institution. Even a philosopher like Plato, who was clearly much influenced by Socrates, believed that a love of truth, not an admiration for an individual, should be our motive. Indeed, it is generally accepted that many of Plato's own views were developed beyond anything Socrates had ever said. His own pupil, Aristotle, himself departed from Plato's position in fundamental ways. Yet, despite this, it is ironic that various kinds of 'Platonists' and 'Aristotelians' have, through the centuries, slavishly followed what they interpreted as their respective hero's views.

Debate between philosophers, at its best, can be a dialogue of reason with itself. It is never enough to learn what a particular philosopher thinks, or to be able to give a clear account of a philosophical position. Someone can learn all the arguments of Plato and Aristotle, or of more recent philosophers. That of itself does not produce a philosopher or even an ability to think philosophically. The important task is to engage with the issues for oneself, and to decide what one agrees with and what one repudiates. This must be done on a rational basis, and not through the unthinking application of one's own prejudices, or those of one's time and place. It is hardly surprising that it is difficult, if not impossible, to be both a consistent relativist and a philosopher. The former relates everything to its own social context. The latter appeals to a reason that transcends the immediate circumstances that so clearly influence us. It aspires to some kind of universal validity. The relativist will insist that all rationality is itself situated in, and limited to, particular historical periods. Yet repudiating a reason that can transcend history will only mean that we are trapped in our own historical period. We will share its assumptions and have no basis for questioning them. In the same way, an appeal to reason raises problems for the convinced materialist. If everything is just 'body', or whatever contemporary science claims are the basic constituents of physical reality, what is reason? Is it just neural connections being set up in the brain? Once again, rationality seems to be questioned. Is it just the arbitrary behaviour of atoms, as the pre-Socratic atomists thought? Could it be explained by the behaviour of sub-atomic particles, as contemporary physicists might be inclined to think?

Progress in Philosophy

Both a global relativism rooting everything in its social contexts, and a literally mindless materialism, sweeping aside everything that cannot be understood in material form, arose in ancient Athens. Yet both doctrines are flourishing as never before, at the start of the twenty-first century, although it is actually very hard to combine them. Forms of materialism claim truth and would not be content with relativism. Relativists could only allow materialism as one of any number of the beliefs of different societies. The fact that Socrates and Plato were dealing with what appeared to be the same issues as are current today, itself gives the lie to any idea that each society has its own standards of thought, or its own criteria of what reasoning is. If we can stretch across the centuries, and even the millennia, to take hold of what Plato says, that suggests that both he and we are not just mere creations of particular societies. Philosophy is not just mere prejudice springing from a particular historical context. He and we, it could be argued, share in a common rationality that can allow communication, despite the obvious differences in our situations.

Modern forms of materialism and of relativism are bound to confront us in any inquiry about the nature of the world and how we can know it. What is the world we live in really like, no matter how it appears? Linked with this issue is the equally important question as to how knowledge of the world is even possible. The former, in philosophers' language, is a question of ontology, of reasoning about what there is. The latter is a matter of epistemology concerning the basis of human knowledge. One of the most vexed questions in philosophy is the relation between the two. Some would not see that there is a difference. After all, we cannot talk of what we do not know. How, then, can questions about reality be separated from questions about our knowledge? There is, however, much more to be said, not least because questions about knowledge have to be, at least in part, about us and our capabilities.

Talk about Plato and his contemporaries may help to set the scene for a philosophical discussion. It shows that philosophy is not a recent phenomenon, but that it deals with questions that have been with us since the dawn of Western civilization. The minute that thinkers wanted reasons and were not content with the kind of myths Homer told in his poetry, about gods misbehaving, philosophy was born. The very distinction between myth and reason ('logos' in Greek) lay at the heart of Greek philosophy. This shows the venerable age of philosophy as a discipline. Does it not, however, show something less attractive? A cynic may ask why, if questions have been debated so long, is agreement no nearer now than in Plato's time? Science undoubtedly progresses, or so many claim. In the twenty-first century, physics will presumably progress even more, and perhaps produce a 'grand unified theory'. That, it is hoped, will be universally accepted, and will unlock the mysteries of the physical universe, unifying our knowledge of it. Why, then, does no one seriously suggest that any such thing will happen in philosophy? Similarly, scientists like pointing out to philosophers that in their disciplines there is no such thing as 'French biology', 'German physics' or 'Anglo-American science'. Yet applying such adjectives to philosophy may not seem so ridiculous. Science claims universality and in fact does achieve universal recognition. Why then does philosophy glory in its labels? Why does there seem to be no such thing as philosophical progress? Philosophers do not appear to know more now than their predecessors did in Athens. Perhaps the celebration of its ancient past merely underlines a basic weakness in philosophy.

These are important issues, although, in so far as they are talking about the nature of knowledge and truth, they seem themselves to be of a philosophical nature. We cannot escape philosophy once we start questioning ourselves and our assumptions, or our beliefs and our practices. Yet although philosophy may be inescapable, some may wish it were more obviously successful. What is at stake here is the legitimacy of the comparison between philosophy as a discipline and science as one. That itself involves us in examining the philosophical presuppositions of science. Science itself, despite its social prestige, cannot be taken at face value. Philosophy should not be too ready to accept scientific standards of success. Answers do not come ready packaged, once we are talking of profound questions about the nature of the world we live in and our relation to it. We are confronted by the limitations and fallibility of human understanding, as well as by its abilities and successes. Indeed, philosophy can prove a useful antidote to the arrogance which can be produced by dwelling on apparent scientific progress. Humans may be much more in control of their physical environment than they used to be. It is unclear how far they are in control of themselves. Philosophy can remind us that when we confront basic questions concerning our place in the scheme of things, and our relation to physical reality, our understanding is still limited. Just because humans have always found some questions difficult, and perhaps for that reason sometimes prefer not to ask them, that does not mean the questions and answers are not important. Indeed if, as seems inevitable, even science depends on philosophical presuppositions, we cannot achieve success in science without making philosophical assumptions about the nature of the world which the scientist is investigating.

Philosophy and the World

Anyone who begins to study philosophy discovers quickly that there is no obvious body of knowledge to be learnt. It is a method of thinking, rather than a collection of facts. That is not to say that one should not know what great philosophers have taught in the past, or what philosophers are arguing about in the present day. Yet knowing what is received opinion among a collection of philosophers is not as relevant to philosophical thought itself as the agreed views of the leaders of a scientific discipline would be for those who want to become expert in that science. Indeed, philosophy must be very ready to point out that even agreement in science has to be tentative and provisional. Agreement in any field does not constitute truth. The history of the world is full of examples of people who have been individually and collectively certain of their position, and yet been proved wrong. Certainty is no infallible guide to truth. If we all agreed, as once people did, that the earth is flat, that would not mean that it is so. Even if I am absolutely certain about something, that does not guarantee its truth. No doubt there have been people who, in moments of derangement, have been convinced that they were Napoleon, or even perhaps a fried egg. That, however, says something about them and their current state, and nothing about what is really the case.

Philosophers, therefore, can take nothing for granted, and anyone thinking philosophically should not be reassured by a growing consensus. Even unfashionable views in philosophy, as elsewhere, may be right. Truth can never be arrived at by counting heads. Yet this is all very well, it may be said, but how then can we ever obtain knowledge? Granted that mere agreement is not enough, how can we find out what we ought to agree about? We must, in the end, be constrained by the nature of the world, which we all live in. If I believe it is not raining when it is, I will still get wet when I go out. If I live on the thirty-second floor, getting out through the window will still not prove to be a safe way of leaving the building. In other words, whatever we, or others, may believe, the important point is not that we think something, but the nature of what we think. The crucial point about beliefs is not so much that they are ours. They must at least purport to be about something independent of the belief. Whether or not they are true is then a matter of what the world is like.

Another way of putting this is that truth is not constituted either by private certainty or public agreement. It is an objective matter and is connected with the object of belief. It is a matter of what the belief is supposed to be about rather than who holds it. Objectivity is a matter of being connected with the nature of things, rather than of the attitudes that people hold. Only what is real can be a genuine source of truth. What then is real? What kind of things should we be looking for? We must have some conception of what the world is really like.

There have always been philosophers who have resisted this radical separation of the subject and object of belief. The emphasis on the importance of the objective reality of the world, and its independence from human judgement, has been challenged from several directions. Above all, 'idealists' have wanted to hold that reality is dependent on mind, although that does not necessarily mean the human mind. Bishop Berkeley, in the eighteenth century, wanted to ground reality in the mind of God. To be, he thought, was to be perceived. Since he believed that God perceives everything, this does not cause as much of a problem as might be thought. Even so, the world, that is everything, only exists as far as it is known and perceived by God. It has no independent existence. God does not know it because it exists. It exists because God knows it.

More sceptical philosophies would not presume to bring God into the picture in the first place. Those of an idealist persuasion would link reality to human understanding. They would stress the central importance of the human mind. This, however, seems to make whatever exists, including the physical world, depend on human judgement. That makes the whole universe revolve around human beings in a logical, if not literal, sense. What exists only does so in so far as we think it does. Everything is centred on us. It is anthropocentric. Common sense would reject this as a ludicrous conception, but we must be careful, since, as we have already noted, common sense is likely merely to recapitulate the views of earlier generations of philosophers.

Most people in their everyday lives, like most working scientists, do not think of the world as a projection of their minds. They do not imagine that we are living in a dream of our own creation, even if it is one that others share. They assume that sticks and stones, tables and chairs, and, more controversially, electrons and other sub-atomic particles, are 'really there'. These things help to form the context in which we live our lives. The physical world constrains us. It is not always like walking into a brick wall when we thought there was a door there. Nevertheless, we all have experience of the world not conforming to our wishes. It is 'there', resisting, and not as malleable as we would sometimes wish. We cannot control it by thought. Indeed, it sometimes seems to be controlling us. Many would agree with the 'argument' of the venerable Dr Johnson against idealism. He is said to have kicked a stone and exclaimed: 'I refute it thus!' Needless to say, the philosophical arguments in its favour are too subtle to be dismissed so easily, and idealism constantly reappears in new forms. They constantly trade on the simple fact that we cannot think or talk about what we cannot think or talk about. Thought and language can then seem not just a means of access to reality. They can appear to have a major role in forming it.

The resistance of the world can lead easily to the view that what is real is whatever is physical. This means that what is real is not just what can be seen, touched, or otherwise experienced. That keeps too close a link between reality and experience. It is simply what physics deals with. Calling it 'matter' does not necessarily help, since matter itself seems difficult to define in contemporary science. It seems almost to disappear into energy. Certainly it is not composed of indivisible atoms, since each atom itself contains innumerable particles. It seems difficult to get down to bits of stuff, which could be imagined perhaps as little billiard balls knocking into each other or sticking together in various ways. Scientists and philosophers once thought like this, but modern physics makes such a simple picture impossible. The term 'materialist', therefore, is not very helpful, and many philosophers prefer to talk of 'physicalism'. That deals with whatever physics accepts, while 'naturalism' could be understood as accepting more generally what is within the scope of the natural sciences as a whole. In this way, 'reality', a typically philosophical concept, suddenly becomes linked with contemporary science. This is not an oversight.

Many philosophers have come to feel that the methods of science alone can be a guarantee of knowledge. This is partly because of the undoubted success of science in helping us to predict, control and manipulate the physical world. Many are highly suspicious of anything beyond the scope of physics, and feel that once the constraint of empirical investigation is ignored, anyone can claim anything. The floodgates of superstition are thereby opened, together with every form of fanciful belief. For such people, philosophy should be the servant of the sciences, clarifying and systematizing their methods. It cannot then be thought of as an independent source of knowledge, or as an alternative method of investigation.

There are no philosophical laboratories, no philosophical experiments and no accumulation of philosophical knowledge in the manner of the sciences. Philosophers do not sift out experience through testing and experimenting. Philosophy is not an empirical discipline. It does not seem to depend on what we can discover about the world around us. Yet the crux is whether that means it cannot be concerned with truth. Certainly, throughout the history of philosophy, a place has been given for 'metaphysics', a study of reality transcending the world of appearance, or the ordinary world we experience. Metaphysics has never taken things at face value, and indeed is like modern science in looking for deeper explanations behind the ordinary world of sights and sounds. Part of the reason for making philosophy subservient to science is fear of the alternative. If philosophy is given its traditional place as the grounding for all other knowledge, we could easily begin referring to entities beyond the scope of science. Metaphysics can encourage talk of realities that do not merely 'transcend' physical reality, but are invisible, intangible, and in fact apparently totally undetectable.

2

Science and the World

Empiricism

Whether or not modern science has a monopoly on knowledge, it has acquired a growing influence over the past three and a half centuries. This itself has had its effect on philosophy, and nowhere is the connection of philosophy with science more apparent than in the philosophical doctrine of empiricism. It was put forward, in particular, by the three great British empiricist philosophers, John Locke, George Berkeley and David Hume, in the seventeenth and eighteenth centuries. They each came from different backgrounds. Locke, originally from Somerset, began as an Oxford philosopher, and was to play a significant role in public affairs around the time of the 'Glorious Revolution' of 1688. Berkeley was a churchman, a bishop in the Anglican Church of Ireland. Hume was a leader of the Scottish Enlightenment in Edinburgh. They all took science seriously and encouraged a concentration on what can be experienced.

Hume took this to great lengths, to the extent that he became worried about what a cause is. We only ever see one event followed by another. How can we be sure that there is some link between them? We may associate the two happenings in our minds, but is there more to it than that? Causation can appear to be no more than the constant conjunction of events. We strike a match and a flame appears. The question that concerned Hume is whether we merely associate the two, or whether there is some unobservable power in nature which produces the effect. Similarly, Hume was unsure how we could know that the future will resemble the past. Just because our experiences have run to a pattern and, for example, we find that the sun rises every day, this seems no absolute guarantee that this will continue. Science tends to assume regularity in nature, an inherent order. A true empiricist would have to say that all we can be sure of is that we have discovered, or appeared to discover, regularities up to now. Everything may change tomorrow. This is the problem of induction, going from the known to the unknown, the seen to the unseen, or the past to the future. In fact, an extreme empiricist might only be able to claim knowledge from present experience. Even the past becomes problematic and potentially inaccessible. Hume was sceptical about the existence of God, and could not appeal to God as the source of order in the world. Locke, on the other hand, was a firm believer in the Christian God. He was able to appeal to God as the source of order and rationality in the world. Yet he was also regarded as the founder of British empiricism, and was an influential figure in the early stages of modern science in the seventeenth century.

Empiricism gained a firmer grip with later developments in Western science. In the last century it gained its most emphatic influence on philosophy through the Vienna Circle, a meeting of science-orientated philosophers in Austria in the 1920s and 1930s. They insisted that truth, and meaning, were to be linked to verification and falsification. In other words, you cannot meaningfully claim anything if you do not know how to check your statement. You have to be able to say what would count for or against it. They meant by verification anything that could be checked by science. Truth, therefore, became by definition a matter wholly for the physical sciences. Metaphysics is ruled out, as is anything that contains an uncheckable truth. It became notorious that the 'logical positivists', as they were called, ruled out the possibility of any claims to truth in such spheres as religion, morality or aesthetics. Science cannot prove the existence of God. It cannot decide on the rightness of a course of activity, the goodness of a person or the beauty of anything. It seemed to follow that God, goodness, duty and beauty were not part of the fabric of the world. This kind of view was popularized in English by A. J. Ayer in his book, *Language, Truth and Logic*. He attended meetings of the Vienna Circle, as did the prominent American philosopher, W. V. Quine. The latter dominated much of American philosophy in the second half of the twentieth century. For Quine, there was, as he put it, no 'first philosophy', no metaphysics.

One area in which Quine did part company with the positivists was the way in which he allowed a much greater role for theory in science. Hume's empiricism found it difficult to stray from immediate experience. Quine based his philosophy on science, but accepted that scientific theories could posit entities, which may not be immediately available to scientific investigators. A true empiricist has always found it difficult to envisage unobservable entities, such as sub-atomic particles. Indeed, at a time when the other side of the moon had not yet been directly observed there seemed to be a problem in talking of an undoubted reality, like that, when we could not observe it. A wedge had thus to be driven between reality and the possibility of verification. What was real was not just what was within the reach of scientists. It was also, everyone recognized, what was in principle within reach. In other words, we might not be able to check something, but we would know what it would be to do so. There was still a contrast between something that could eventually be observed and something totally unobservable. What, for instance, would be your reaction if I claimed that there were goblins in my garden? The only problem, I could say, is that they were so shy that they would run away every time anyone went looking for them. The result would be that they were never seen. They also, I might say, worked very hard, but since goblin work is always undetectable by humans, I could not show you the difference that they made. You might then ask what they looked like. Since I had never seen any, I would not be able to tell you. Exasperated, you would then quite rightly wish to know how I had any inkling that they were there in the first place. You would not be too impressed if I said that I could not give any reasons or appeal to any evidence. 'I just know', I might say.

However, it is surprising how much apparent human knowledge cannot be directly checked by an immediate verification, and yet is not entirely baseless. One problem is what will count as evidence or a reason for belief in the first place. The logical positivists narrowed 'evidence' to such an intolerable extent that even physical science itself could not function according to their demanding standards. Reducing reality to what can be directly experienced by humans changes the subject in a dramatic way. The focus moves from whatever exists to how we experience it, from reality to human knowledge of it, from metaphysics to epistemology. The result is that we turn our attention to the capabilities and limitations of the investigator instead of being preoccupied with what we are investigating. We thus have to become more concerned with scientists, and what they can do, than with the objects of their research.

It is vital that if reality is linked to science we know exactly what we mean by science. The example of the other side of the moon in the 1950s suggests that we cannot just take science as it is at any one moment and think that it defines reality. Science progresses, it appears, accumulating and extending knowledge. It certainly changes and sometimes these changes can take a radical form, as when quantum mechanics replaced classical mechanics: suddenly the world did not appear to be operating according to mechanistic laws; at the deepest physical level, events were seen to be unpredictable, undetermined and even random. We can never afford to assume that science has given its last word on an issue. If we are not careful, we can easily push this line of thinking too far, and imagine that because science is provisional in nature, nothing it says tells us about the real world at all. Some people regard scientific theories as just the outcome of particular social contexts. This is an extreme view that is just as mistaken as it is to think that the science of the present day is an infallible source of knowledge. Science is revisable and will be revised. Its conclusions, however well established they appear to be, must always be regarded as to some extent provisional and tentative.

The Authority of Science

How much authority, then, should science have, given that its conclusions may be wrong? When politicians try to pass the responsibility for a tricky issue, like genetic engineering, to scientists, they are prone to use phrases such as 'science says', as if science contains rock-solid knowledge which is complete and can never be queried or questioned. The history of science, even of the last hundred years, shows this is far from the case. It is constantly developing and conclusions drawn at any one time must be treated with care. Human beings are not omniscient and most science has to extrapolate from inadequate evidence. As a result, when scientists say that there is no evidence that beef supplies, mobile phones or a particular form of genetic engineering are harmful, they mean precisely what they say. They have no evidence. That does not mean that any of these things are not harmful, any more than that they are. We just do not know. Obviously the absence of evidence is encouraging, but it does not itself entirely prove safety. The claim that there is no evidence that a particular food is dangerous is not at all the same as saying that the food is safe. People naturally make the transition from one to the other. Yet the first claim is about our state of knowledge (or ignorance), and that could change. The second is much more clearly about the world rather than about us. There is a deep dispute in philosophy about the precise difference. Can we distinguish talk of the world as it is in itself from a world built up from the empirical evidence at our disposal? Those who stress the world as it is in itself are called 'realists'. They feel that the notion of an objective reality, independent of our understanding of it, cannot be redefined. Reality cannot become a reality merely seen from our point of view.

Once it is accepted that reality, whatever its nature, is distinct from our perception and understanding of it, materialism becomes much more speculative as a doctrine. Many materialists would be surprised at this statement, since they are 'realist' by inclination themselves. They are saying that whatever we may think, the only real things are material. We may feel inclined only to believe in what we can hear, touch, smell, and above all see, but contemporary science takes us far beyond this. The view that only the material can be real becomes a metaphysical doctrine, making claims about what lies far outside our experience. Nevertheless, it might be claimed, scientific methodology must remain authoritative. We can only understand the world, it may seem, through its rigorous discipline. Many would insist that there has to be some connection between the way we see the world scientifically and what we take the character of the world to be. Yet do we really wish to link reality to the way present-day science leads us to think? We should at least think of science as it one day will be, when we have much further information about the world than we do at present. How far ahead should we look – ten years or perhaps a hundred? The American pragmatist philosopher, C. S. Peirce, suggested that we should speak of a scientific millennium, when all the facts are in, and science at last reaches a fixed and settled state. He was writing towards the end of the nineteenth century, and science seems no more likely to reach that condition at the beginning of the twenty-first century than it did then. It seems distinctly hypothetical, especially given human limitations and fallibility. It has to be an aspiration, or a 'regulative ideal', rather than something we can imagine will actually happen. Perhaps an ideal science is something which any rational being with complete information would produce. This, however, is itself so hypothetical as to be indistinguishable from pure metaphysics. It does not even seem so very different from defining reality in terms of the omniscience of God.

Making reality dependent on some actual or possible scientific discovery seems to lose any clear point when we realize that human science is so limited, partly because of our own location in the universe. Physicists are fond of distinguishing between the 'observable' and 'unobservable' universe. The latter is, in principle, bound to be beyond our reach because of the way the universe has expanded. That does not of itself mean that it does not exist. We have to make a decision as to whether we think physical laws apply in regions far beyond those we could ever be familiar with. Some physicists, indeed, see the development of the universe, in the words of one, as ' the result of contingent and historical processes of self-organization, rather than being imposed by absolute and pre-existing law'.[1] This would mean that facts about the world are contingent. They do not have to be as they are and could have been otherwise. Indeed, in different physical regions they might well be different even now. The issue is whether a principle of rationality has to be understood as imposed on the world from a source outside it, such as God.

Might different physical processes organize themselves differently, so that there could be alternative systems of physical laws? Views of an evolving cosmos may come to this position, even though it is very far from Plato's vision of one world reflecting one set of absolute standards. The argument is that 'the Platonic conception of law as mathematical and eternal must give way to a view in which the laws are themselves formed as a result of a process of evolution or self-organization'.[2] The notion of an absolute law cannot be accepted unexamined. Yet the idea of many alternative sets of laws, possibly all operating somewhere, can result in the conception of innumerable 'universes', all by definition unconnected with each other and all operating in a totally different way. The physicist Lee Smolin speculates that black holes may be the source of other universes. He says: 'As our own visible universe contains an enormous number of black holes, there must be enormous numbers of these other universes'.[3] This is only one example of a tendency in physics to talk of many worlds, sometimes linked to, or parallel with, this one, and sometimes wholly different.

The idea that there are many universes with different sets of laws is at the moment virtually the orthodox position among cosmologists. The view graphically illustrates the contingency of physical laws, holding that the physical world is not inevitable and does not have to be the way it is. Too much stress on laws has always tended to suggest that some iron necessity dictates the way things are. The association of such laws either with God, or with mathematics, has helped reinforce the idea that such laws are inevitable because, in some sense, necessary. On the other hand, talk of such 'laws' may be merely shorthand for referring to the tendencies, regularities and propensities which we find in nature. Indeed even reference to God does not imply that He had to create a world in one way rather than another. Suggesting that limits His omnipotence. God must be seen as being able to will freely, as He chooses.

Bringing in the idea of many universes is a graphic way of showing that this world, with its particular set of physical constants, is only one possibility.

Empiricism has been remorselessly drawn away from the easy connection of reality with immediate experience, and has to deal with possible experience. It must come to terms with undoubted limitations on the extent of human knowledge. Logical positivism respected physics as the foundation of all science, but physics, in reaching out to the unobservable, has ironically caused problems for a simple empiricism. Yet this provides an interesting test case for the relations of philosophy and science. The question is whether philosophy must accept whatever physical speculation comes up with. Does science in general, and physics in particular, have to be constrained by philosophy? Arguments about the interpretation of quantum mechanics lead rapidly into philosophical arguments between realists and empiricists. They cannot decide how far a sub-atomic reality exists apart from the fact of our measurements in an experimental situation. Arguments about the possibility of many universes must also take on a philosophical character. Once we step beyond what can be directly observed, measured or tested, we are on the verge of going beyond the physical to the metaphysical. The idea that scientists must have the last word on a subject just because they are scientists, and that philosophers must meekly follow behind, is not in fact the brake on superstition and wild speculation that it might appear to be. Goblins in one's garden might appear to be comparatively harmless compared with the multiplication of universes.

Many Universes

When physicists say that there could be other types of universe, much depends on what is meant by 'universe'. If there is more than one, it must be assumed they are not in contact with each other, nor able to influence one another. The point is that they will, presumably, be operating according to very different laws, otherwise there is little point in referring to different universes, as opposed to different regions of the same one. Another universe must be totally inaccessible from ours, with its processes totally unlike those with which we are familiar. The very idea of the 'physical' is being strained if its 'physical' laws cannot be understood in terms of our physics. In fact, asserting the existence of another universe with a physical constitution totally dissimilar from that of our own, must have little basis in physics. The assertion of its existence seems a good example of a metaphysical belief. It cannot be substantiated, even in principle, by any possible scientific investigation on our part.

One reason for talking of many universes in physics has stemmed from the so-called 'anthropic principle'. This has been put forward since the 1970s by eminent physicists such as John Wheeler, a pupil of Einstein and the originator of the term 'black hole'. They have drawn attention to the way that the physical preconditions for life in general, and human life in particular, appear to have been built into the very first moments of the development of the universe. The universe could not have developed in such a way as to sustain life if some physical constants had been infinitesimally different. Only very specific circumstances could have eventually allowed the forming of carbon-based life like ours. As has been graphically said, we are composed of the ashes of stars. Billions of years, and very precise initial conditions, were needed for carbon-producing stars even to have been formed. Even though, by definition, we could not find ourselves in a universe inhospitable to human life, should we not be surprised that the only universe which has evolved is one that could produce intelligent creatures like us? It may look as if it had all been intended. Indeed, some have been tempted to produce from the anthropic principle an argument from the design of the universe to the existence of God. Should, on the other hand, the development of the universe be explained wholly in terms of physical processes? The problem is that if the latter is the case, it seems unlikely that any one possibility should have been explored. The reason that we find ourselves in this universe may not seem so extraordinary if there are many universes. There would no doubt be innumerable ones unable to support life in the way that we know it. One might suppose, indeed, that all possibilities would have been realized.

One possibility is to accept that the uniqueness of this universe is a brute fact. No further explanation is needed. Philosophers through the ages who have wanted to see purpose in everything would not be happy with this. Yet the multiplication of universes does little to give a real explanation as to why we exist in this universe. Of course, if all possible universes are actualized it may not be particularly surprising that one of them can support life. There will, after all, be a vast array. The production of all of them is random and purposeless, but since we are, by definition, amongst the possibilities (since we know we exist), here we are. This, however, seems an extravagant answer to the problem. If the answer to some issue is to appeal to an infinite number of universes, all unconnected with each other, we could not have been given a more complicated answer. We must be in desperate straits if the solution to any problem is an infinite number of universes.

Whatever its faults, the attraction of the verification principle of the logical positivists can become apparent. As a criterion of meaning, it is hopeless.

Since it cannot itself be verified, it would seem itself meaningless. Nevertheless there must be some check on what we can talk about. It may be wishful thinking to assume that everything is accessible to humans. Talking, though, of whole universes that are in principle inaccessible does raise a profound philosophical question. Why should we do so, when by definition no possible physical evidence for it could ever be forthcoming? If we were to get in communication with an alternative universe, that would merely prove it was not unconnected to ours. It only makes sense to talk of multiple universes if we know that we could never have any scientific reason for believing in their existence. Physicists who talk of alternative universes may think that they are pursuing a firmly physicalist agenda. Other universes, after all, sound solid enough. If, though, they are not physical in our sense, such physicists are being as profoundly metaphysical as any theist who wishes to invoke God. Both are going far beyond what can be tested, even in principle, by science. One difference, indeed, is that much religion does not believe that God is in principle wholly inaccessible from this world. It is often alleged that He can reveal Himself within it.

The appeal to many universes is often an explicit alternative to an appeal to God as creator. The assumption is that if all possibilities are actual somewhere, then we need no special explanation in terms of a creator for the existence of our own environment. Arguments rage as to which is the simpler form of reasoning. Some would claim that the appeal to one entity (if God is 'an entity') is preferable to an appeal to many, let alone an infinite number. Others would argue, in a physicalist or naturalist manner, that many universes are examples of the same type of thing. It is, therefore, less extravagant, they would allege, to talk of different 'tokens' or instances of the same type, than to start talking about a very different kind of 'Being'. Anything that marks a distinction between the natural and the supernatural, or the physical and the non-physical, appears to bring in reference to a radically different type of thing. Some would therefore conclude that it is simpler, and therefore preferable, to believe in many universes rather than in one God. Theists would retort that postulating an infinite number of anything, or supposing that all possibilities have to be realized, could not be a good example of simplicity. It is better, they would argue, to look for an explanation in terms of the one universe we know rather than myriads we do not. In any case, they would add, the mere actualization of possibilities does not solve anything. The fact that there are many universes might lessen our surprise at being in one of them. It does nothing to explain why any of them exist in the first place. Why does this universe exist? Because many do, it will be said. Why do the many exist? If there were some ultimate mechanism for producing universes, we are not far from what some people have meant by God, as the ground of everything. The big divide will still be between those who see a personal God acting for reasons and having purposes, and those who look for an impersonal ground operating mechanically without intention or design.

The suspicion remains that the arguments about many universes are often ultimately theological or anti-theological. Many scientists do not like cosmic coincidences, which look as if they have been designed. Such coincidences may seem less remarkable if they are just one of an infinite number of possibilities being explored. Yet that itself seems such a curious state of affairs that it demands an explanation. Certainly the 'many universes' view cannot answer the ultimate philosophical question of why there is anything rather than nothing. An infinite number seems no less surprising than one on its own. Indeed it is a state of affairs that may appear even more remarkable.

One thing in all this should be quite clear. These arguments are of their nature philosophical and not scientific. Scientists should not use their considerable social prestige to get us to believe things that make no sense from a philosophical point of view. No scientific observation, by definition, could show us anything about another universe. If that were the case, as we have stressed, we would be looking merely at an extension of our own. The mere fact that some scientists argue for many universes need not show that the argument has much to do with science. It involves the deepest philosophical issues about what has to be the case, about the undesirability of positing superfluous entities, and about the relevance of simplicity, as a test for truth. In fact, the whole debate about the role of purpose and chance is raised. Finally, it involves the issue as to whether all explanation should be couched in physical terms alone. Might Socrates have been right in wanting to look further at the role of mind in organizing matter? The alternative is ultimate pointlessness, or cosmic absurdity. That, of course, may be just what some scientists prefer. It is still a philosophical issue, and not a scientific one.

Physicalism and Naturalism

William of Ockham (a village in Surrey) was a medieval logician, who wielded what has come to be called 'Ockham's razor'. He believed that one should not multiply superfluous entities. One should prefer forms of explanation which do not involve appeal to extra entities. We should be parsimonious about admitting what exists. If we do not have to appeal to fairies to explain the growth of lettuces, we should not assume that there are fairies in the garden making them grow. This may seem sound advice when we are faced with the spectre of countless universes. It can also be rigorously applied, to pare down existence to the ordinary material entities that are accessible to humans. As we have seen, even contemporary science may not be content with this. What, though, about the more general doctrine that one should only allow the existence of material entities? This tends to be recast into the question as to whether anything beyond the scope of the natural sciences can be assumed to exist. It can be refined into a doctrine of physicalism, which assumes that the only real entities are those that physics can take account of. This may not seem much of a restriction if physics starts generating universes, but it obviously draws a contrast between the 'physical' and the 'non-physical', and by implication between the 'natural' and the 'supernatural'.

Other sciences have to be 'reduced' to physics, if the latter becomes the judge of what is real. Biological processes have to be seen as another way of describing what is really a series of physical events. Cells in an organism, and the organism itself, are merely the product of the behaviour of atoms and, beneath that, of sub-atomic particles. The whole, at whatever level, is then never more than the sum of its parts. Knowing what a thing is becomes a matter of analysing it into its constituent parts down to the level of the smallest elements in reality, the elementary particles. The question of the whole and its parts is a venerable problem which can occur in a wide variety of contexts. You can take a car engine to bits and lay it neatly on the drive in front of the house. Does the engine still exist? If you can put it all together again, assuming you can, is the engine which powers the car no more than the collection of scrap metal that formerly adorned the drive? The question is whether we can say that the components are somehow more real than the engine as a whole.

Many think that there is an advantage in unifying everything in one system of explanation. There will be one basic explanation for all the differences apparent in the world, if only everything can be taken to pieces until one reaches the same substratum. There will be a common unity explaining the variety, and it is thought that physics holds the key to it. The motive is not so very different from that of the pre-Socratic philosophers, who looked for a principle of unity underlying all the apparent change in the world. Nowadays, scientists do not look to a particular substance, such as air, fire or water, each of which was proposed as the basic principle of reality by different philosopher-scientists just before the time of Socrates. Instead, physicists hanker for a set of mathematical equations which will uncover the behaviour of energy at its most fundamental level. It is perhaps ironic that even a prominent biologist, E. O. Wilson, advocates the primacy of physics. He was the founder of so-called 'sociobiology', the study of the effect of genes on behaviour. He argues for the view that 'there is intrinsically only one class of explanation'.[4] He talks of uniting the different disciplines in science in what he terms 'consilience'. Yet in all this, physics is to have priority. He says: 'The central idea of the consilience world view was that all tangible phenomena, from the birth of stars to the workings of social institutions, are based on material processes that are ultimately reducible, however long and tortuous the sequences, to the laws of physics.'

This raises the issues as to what is to be precisely understood by the laws of physics, and what reduction involves. Since Wilson, however, makes no secret of his materialism, he is clearly engaged in a programme to demonstrate that the only genuine realities must be explicable in terms acceptable to physics. Even ethical precepts, he suggests, are 'likely to be physical products of the brain and culture'.[5] When, therefore, he suggests that certain things are 'based on' material processes, there is a question as to the role these processes are playing. A genuine materialist will hold that they are the only things that are real. Everything else has to be explained in terms of them.

Wilson is somewhat careless in his use of language in the passage we have just quoted. Whatever the birth of stars or the working of social institutions may involve, they are certainly not tangible. None of us can touch the institution of Parliament, as opposed to the building in which it is housed, any more than we can get our hands on the origin of a star. Yet a materialist will naturally want to assimilate everything, whether far-off physical events or abstract social meanings, to the everyday world of medium-sized physical objects. The world of physics can be made to appear very strange and far removed from the world we experience as humans. Philosophers of science have found it progressively more difficult to relate the world posited by scientific theory to our ordinary everyday experience. Contemporary physics can itself seem very metaphysical in the way it talks of objects far removed from our normal senses.

A materialist, or physicalist, will want to insist on the 'causal closure' of the physical world. In other words, the physical world has to be explained in its own terms, without appeal to external agency or ghostly entities. We shall return to the role of the human mind in all this. Some have always been tempted to see the mental as wholly distinct from the physical. Whatever the philosophical arguments for and against this division into two kinds of reality (often called 'dualism'), many may feel that science itself has to assume a materialist or naturalist position to go about its work. Even if science does not restrict itself to physics, it may still wish to confine reality to what is acceptable to some form of science, otherwise it may have to accept that crucial explanations may be outside its grasp. So-called 'naturalism' may not be very different from physicalism in what it rules out, but it may pursue a less wholehearted reductionist policy within science. It might, for instance, concede that biology has a role in describing entities and that they cannot be reduced to narrowly physical terms. Cells are not the same as sub-atomic particles.

Like physicalism, naturalism is not encumbered by old-fashioned ideas of matter. It is still able to hold that there is nothing in principle beyond the scope of science. The explanation for the world and its processes should not be searched for outside the world. The idea of the supernatural has to be discarded. It is, in fact, very difficult to formulate what exactly is being asserted here, given scientists' willingness to talk of alternative worlds, with different physical laws, which science can never reach. Naturalism, and physicalism, seem to be just contemporary versions of the same old materialism which is more intent on ruling out things such as mind, spirit and God, than in being clear about what it is willing to accept. It is true, though, that science must restrict itself to what it can properly look for. Ockham's razor is not just an instrument to guard against extravagant metaphysics. It helps to keep science focused. Physics, by definition, will not flourish if it too easily gives up its search for physical explanations. Only through empirical research, for example, on the working of the brain, will we be able to understand better how that works. Science may have to adopt a so-called 'methodological naturalism', concentrating on the kind of explanations and entities which it can properly entertain. This is, however, far from being a metaphysical position about what can exist. According to the latter, there is not even a possibility of anything breaking into the self-contained, mechanistic world it assumes to exist. There is then by definition no 'mystery', nothing beyond the scope of human intelligence, and nothing which involves different levels of reality beyond the physical. The world has been 'demystified' and its workings lie ready to be explained in whole.

Notes

1   Lee Smolin, *The Life of the Cosmos*, Weidenfeld and Nicolson, London, 1997, p. 259.
2   Ibid., p. 16.
3   Ibid., p. 93.
4   E. O.Wilson, *Consilience*, Alfred A. Knopf, New York, 1998, p. 266.
5   Ibid., p. 250.

3

Can We Understand the World?

Science and Reason

Philosophy typically involves standing back from ourselves and what we think, and subjecting the very foundations of our thought to critical scrutiny. Even this account involves philosophical presuppositions. Can we really, for instance, detach ourselves from our thinking in this way? Is there such a thing as pure reason, uncontaminated by prejudice or bias? Some would argue that the quest for such 'objective' thought is itself doomed to failure. We cannot step away from every available viewpoint and claim that somehow we have a better view. Many would doubt that there could be a 'view from nowhere', to use a phrase of the American philosopher, Thomas Nagel.

This idea of dispassionate rationality, seeing reality for what it is, often appears to be a product of the European Enlightenment. Many would see it unequivocally as a product of the seventeenth and eighteenth centuries. However, the pursuit of reason and the spirit of detached criticism have deeper roots in ancient Greece. Reason is not a mere cultural product of modern Europe. It cannot be equated simply with the development of the modern world. There are grounds for seeing it as a necessary constituent of any intellectual activity. Subsistence farming may not give many opportunities for deep reflection, but the growth of civilization has always brought sufficient leisure for some people to ask questions about what they are doing and why they are doing it. Even this, however, is to make too clear a distinction between different kinds of society. From the very earliest time, anyone who has looked up at the stars on a clear and frosty night, and wondered about their nature and origin, has begun to reason about our place in the scheme of things. In these days of light pollution, artificial lighting from towns and cities is so strong that the sky reflects their lights from miles away. It is perhaps difficult to capture the elementary wonder of just looking at the sparkling night sky in the pitch black.

Socrates tells the story of the Thracian servant girl who laughed at Thales, the first philosopher.[1] The story – the forerunner of those about absent-minded professors – tells how Thales was so intent on looking up to study the stars that he fell down a well. The servant girl mocked him, saying that he was so eager to see what was in the sky that he could not see what was at his feet. Socrates comments that any who give their lives to philosophy are going to face such mockery. They are going to be so intent on human nature that, as Socrates suggests, they will not know what their neighbours are doing, or even whether they are human. They are, in other words, concentrating on the abstract and on general principles. Those who are more down-to-earth will always find it irritating and prefer to keep with the concrete and the familiar. They will find scholarly detachment and rational thought an unnecessary luxury.

That does not mean that philosophy is dispensable. Some refuse to stand back from their thoughts or practices in order to examine them, but merely get on with their lives. They are always taking something for granted. The appeal to reason is an appeal to a standard which everyone, in all circumstances, can accept. As such, it involves questioning even our most cherished beliefs and standing up to arbitrary authority or challenging tradition. Just because we all live in the same world, we should all have access to the same information and modes of reasoning. We should look to standards of proof, and evidence, to establish conclusions which everyone can accept.

This is certainly a central ideal of modern science. Perhaps we take it too easily for granted that science can claim validity across the world. Physical laws are supposed to hold throughout the universe. Science is about reality and we all confront the same reality. There cannot be local variations in what is acceptable scientifically. Science concerns one world. In other areas of human experience, however, we find it much easier to acknowledge the strength of local tradition, or to recognize that there are different sources of authority. Even in religion, which should surely claim universal truth, the Pope's authority is limited to Catholics. We do not find it strange that an appeal to the Koran carries little weight in the Southern United States. Political authority is in an even worse condition. It does not even pretend to have any universal validity. No one expects the Parliament at Westminster to make rulings for Kansas, any more than the actions of the American Congress are relevant in Outer Mongolia. Bitter fights have occurred over precisely how far the writ of a particular ruler, or legislature, can run. Struggles for independence have revolved around precisely this issue. Yet no one has usually thought that one can or should be 'independent' of the findings of science. We may decide, as many territories of the British Empire did, that we do not wish to be ruled by Westminster any longer. We cannot decide that science does not apply to us. Water boils at one hundred degrees centigrade at sea level, whether we wish it to or not. We cannot vote what reality should be like.

This presupposes that science is somehow in a privileged position, that there is a scientific viewpoint of the world that sees it as it is. In other words, it assumes that rational detachment is possible, and that it is particularly exemplified in the methods of science. Perhaps it is even identical with them. It does not just take for granted that there is one world. It assumes that we can understand the world and that science offers the way. In the eighteenth century, admiration for reason gave a powerful impetus to the development of science. It had a wider social effect as well. Science seemed to be the product of a rational process, to which everyone had access. It gave people a way to truth without apparently having to consult authorities, or merely following in the ways in which they had been brought up. Anyone was free to believe anything, as long as it could be given rational foundations. Freedom and reason were linked and autonomy became the watchword. Traditional thinking, even traditional philosophy, was challenged, merely because it was traditional. Everyone had to see the truth for themselves.

This was linked in many people's minds with ideas of liberation. Reason, it was thought, would free us of the shackles of superstition, often seen by atheists as being provided by the Roman Catholic Church. Reason would bring enlightenment and knowledge. It would bring progress. In fact, reason was often enthroned, almost literally, in the place of God. In France, after the Revolution, Christian churches were converted, for a time, to 'Temples of Reason'. Freedom was proclaimed in the place of respect for the authority of the Church. There was no longer respect for tradition, as personified by monarch and aristocracy. Reason, as a source of self-legislation in every person, was given the place of God as law-giver. For philosophers such as Kant, autonomy was seen as the ground of the dignity of human nature, and of every rational nature. Thrusting tradition aside encouraged a belief in the possibility of social progress. Just as we should not be in thrall to what might be regarded as the fossilized wisdom of previous ages, it was thought that we should not try to tie down those who follow us. Otherwise everything would stay the same and progress would be impossible. Linked to the idea of progress was the idea of 'improvement'. Progress was going forward to a destination. Things were going to get better and they would only do so by changing the beliefs and attitudes of the past. These views applied to morality as well as to much else. They appealed to a rationality which was understood to belong to humans before they entered into any social relations. It was not the product of society as such, let alone any particular one. It was the precondition for it.

The Influence of the Enlightenment

Mention of the French Revolution underlines some of the inherent political dangers arising from a belief in freedom. There is a danger in discarding all traditional restraints and challenging all authority. Freedom can degenerate into anarchy unless something is quickly put in the place of tradition, otherwise there would be no restraint on the use of power and no check on brute force. The reason of an individual seems a weak guide unless it can be shared and applied. Moreover, doubts can be expressed about rationalism as a global view. Reason cannot start afresh in every generation. Progress, whatever that might be, always has to be built on earlier achievements. Yet the important point is that the Enlightenment, whatever its more general social influence, undoubtedly helped to produce modern science. The exercise of reason in science owes much to the ideas about the role of reason established in the seventeenth and eighteenth centuries. Science can claim to be disrespectful of authority. The alleged battles between science and the Christian Church over the centuries form part of the mythology of science.

Science, some think, saved us from the dictates of arbitrary authority and the stultifying constraints of tradition. It sets us free, as a force for individual liberation and for social progress. The growth of knowledge brings improvement. All the slogans of the Enlightenment can easily be applied to science. We will be told that science is objective, in that it sees things as they are detached from any particular perspective. Science can claim universality. In fact, the methods of modern science constitute human reason, or so those claim who see science as the sole heir of the Enlightenment. Yet, in one respect, science has established itself in a way that the Enlightenment devotion to reason never managed. The universality of reason was taken for granted. Not only were humans rational, but the power of reason was able, it was hoped, to produce principles of universal application, which could be universally accepted. Yet this proved a forlorn hope in many spheres, whether in religion, morality or politics. Even appeals to human rights can still be much contested at the beginning of the twenty-first century. The concept of such natural rights, existing universally and demanding universal recognition, is very much an Enlightenment one. The fact that two or three centuries later there is still as much disagreement as ever about them does not say much for the feasibility of the Enlightenment conception of rationality.

Some countries may see appeals to rights as a typically Western phenomenon. They do not belittle physics in this way. Human progress might be a dubious idea. Have we really become better since the eighteenth century? Auschwitz is only one of many places which seem to bear powerful witness against this. Many would hold that the issue is not in question in science. They would say that we now know more in every area of science than a hundred, fifty or perhaps even ten years ago. Indeed, as science grows, and built on the effort of previous generations, the growth of human knowledge becomes exponential. Its rate of increase, in other words, itself quickens. Science is universal and it progresses. People take it for granted that what is taken to be traditional wisdom at one time will quickly alter. In contemporary society the 'shelf-life' of knowledge is relatively short. We are, to change the image, on a roller-coaster ride, where tradition is irrelevant and the future has arrived before we have even become accustomed to the present.

Yet all this should make us pause. How can the 'shelf-life' of genuine knowledge be short? What is really being said is that new discoveries are made, and we realize that we did not in fact previously possess knowledge. What is taken for knowledge at one point, is seen to be mistaken or only partially true. If science is on a path to truth, it may improve on previous errors and partial understanding. Truth itself, however, cannot change. What the world is like cannot alter. Our conception of it changes. Science, at any given moment, must always be treated with caution. Its judgements are always provisional. Science, itself, is the product of human, rational judgement. It may presuppose the possibility of detached human reasoning and be the Enlightenment's proudest heir, but it is only as reliable as the human rationality it expresses. As the information available to us and the evidence accessible increases, we would expect the scope of science to be extended. In the end, however, science is a matter of human judgement. It is not a simple matter of mechanically deducing theories from an array of pre-packaged facts.

The alleged objectivity of science depends on a human ability to detach oneself from bias and prejudice. We seem to be back with the idea of science challenging tradition to produce a better future. Yet, as references to the Enlightenment suggest, science is simply part of a powerful tradition, that of a respect for the power of human reason. The desire for empirical evidence, and the refusal to dabble in unproved mystery, is the product of a historically specific view of human reason and its capabilities. Science, for instance, deliberately rejects the relevance of any divine revelation. An equation of reason with the methods of science is the natural result of the later Enlightenment's rejection of religion. As well as being rooted in a particular tradition, this is a philosophical doctrine about the scope of science. It cannot be formed within science itself.

This view of science as pure reason in action has been under criticism for the last generation. Thomas Kuhn did more than anyone to show how science operates with its own traditions, which he termed 'paradigms'. Because of the centrality of theory at every level, no one, least of all in science, can come to the world without preconceptions. If scientists have no idea of what to look for, it is unlikely that they will find anything. Theories are not unlike powerful torches, giving the means of illuminating the area at which they are directed. Without them, scientists stumble around in the dark. The world does not come neatly bundled into different packages as evidence for one theory or another. There are no raw data already labelled as relevant facts. Detectives looking in a garden for clues after a burglary have to use their intelligence. They will not find objects with little stickers saying 'clue'. Scientists are in a similar position. What they can count as evidence depends on what they are looking for, and that depends on the theory with which they are operating. Minds are active. They are not mere passive recipients of whatever happens to come in from outside. We all have to sift and select from the massive amount of information which bombards our senses. We are not the passive recipients of external data already carrying its own meaning. We must always interpret it, consciously or unconsciously. The idea that we do not have to do this was once derided by the philosopher Sir Karl Popper as the 'bucket theory' of the mind.

If experience has to be organized and interpreted, a large question mark must be placed against simpler forms of empiricism. The latter tended to see theories as deductions from experience, rather than as necessary means of making sense of experience. Scientists cannot just look at the world and draw conclusions from it. They have to be trained and to take on trust the knowledge bequeathed by earlier generations. Established theories in science continue to help us interpret present experience. Scientists themselves cannot repudiate all tradition, because they themselves follow one. Each subdivision of science builds up its own preconceptions and expectations, each in turn forging a powerful new tradition. They all rely on past successes and on classical experiments, just as much as a lawyer relies on precedents. They use generally accepted theories. Some sociologists of science have gone as far as to suggest that scientists only reflect their social context, both the narrow one of their discipline and the wider society of which they are part. Any view, however, suggesting that scientists are not in contact with the real world has to undermine science. The latter must be more than a reflection of varying social characteristics. Different scientists operating in different societies should still reach agreement. Yet nowadays the universal claims of science may not be taken at face value. Science operates with implicit philosophical assumptions, and these are being challenged.

Modern science has assumed there is a real world and that scientists can get in contact with it. An alternative position is to see science as a system of myth-building, no different in principle from a belief in Homeric gods. The justification for taking part in scientific practices can only be that they are a disciplined way of helping us to know about the world. Two questions press themselves at this point. First, can science be confident of the power of human reason to understand the world? Second, is it correct to view science as the sole example of such reason? Scientific rationalism has taken the answer to both questions for granted. Without giving answers to them, we may accept science at face value, but we have little scope for facing up to challenges to its intellectual standing. A deep cynicism about the possibility of progress in human affairs has reduced faith in the Enlightenment project, and made people think that change does not necessarily mean progress. Auschwitz itself can seem the outcome of modern technology. The status of science itself can be questioned. It may seem impossible to think that the world has a distinctive nature, or that our minds are especially equipped to understand it.

What Makes Science Successful?

There is a deep suspicion in many quarters about the pursuit of scientific knowledge. The more that science appears to understand and the more it manipulates physical processes, the more problems seem to occur. Science no longer seems to be a universal and unmixed blessing. Global warming and the alleged ensuing interference with weather patterns is one example of an area where people are getting very uneasy. They are afraid that the technological application of scientific knowledge may have unintended consequences. Genetic engineering is another major source of concern. It will have unforeseeable consequences, and nobody knows how beneficial, or harmful, they will be. The more knowledge we acquire, the more problems seem to be caused.

Science is challenged to justify itself. Knowledge certainly does not always bring progress in society. Yet even the claim of science to give us knowledge has to be put under scrutiny. It is another version of the profound philosophical questions of what knowledge is, and how we can acquire it. Is the ability of scientists to control the world a lucky accident? How do we know that we really understand the relevant physical processes? Some people think that science is justified merely because it 'works'. Many scientists believe that they are accomplishing more than that. Science does not just aim for technological wizardry, or control over physical objects. It must be concerned with what is true, with the character of the real world, the processes of which are independent of us. Applied science always depends on pure science. Technology depends on knowledge. Needless to say, any anti-realist philosophy, which says that there is no independent, real world, undermines the apparent purpose and role of science. Without the belief that they are investigating something beyond themselves and their society, scientists cannot do their job.

As well as demanding a realist philosophy, science has to assume the existence of an ordered, regular world, which is, moreover, intelligible to human understanding. None of these characteristics can be taken for granted. The functioning of science demands them. The scientific legacy of the Enlightenment seemed to involve an assumption that human reasoning could unlock the secrets of the universe. It made humans of central importance by stressing their autonomy, but did not answer the question why human reason could get a grip on its surroundings. The ongoing success of science has seemed to carry with it its own guarantee, but philosophy should teach us not to take that kind of thing for granted. The very idea of such 'success' is open to examination. Saying that science 'works' just raises the question of what counts as 'working'. Predictive success and an ability to control our surroundings may be impressive. They are hardly self-evident proofs that we can properly understand physical laws, or their ultimate foundation. The quest for a final theory in physics is still unfinished.

Modern science, as we have said, can trace its origins to seventeenth-century Europe. Its development was inextricably linked with philosophical and theological understanding. The belief in laws of nature was undoubtedly influenced by the idea that God, as creator, had promulgated them. The inherent order of the world was seen as a reflection of the mind and purposes of God. Reading the 'Book of Nature' in a scientific way was to understand the will of God as much as reading that other Book, the Bible. Scientists such as Newton and Boyle, in Cambridge, certainly believed this. They, together with others who helped found the Royal Society in England, were influenced by theological ideas which placed a high value on human reason. Because God was sovereign, God did not have to create the world in a particular way. It was therefore necessary to investigate through empirical methods the true nature of the physical world. It was not enough to reason, as the ancient Greeks were prone to do, about how things must be. They had been drawn to geometry and mathematics rather than experimental science. Modern science was made possible through the realization that it is necessary to investigate the world empirically in order to discover how God in fact had made it. The contingency of the world was a theological idea. Thinking that the world had to be one way rather than another would be to challenge the omnipotence of God. God's will determined everything, and God's creation reflected the divine reason.

Great philosophical battles occurred in the seventeenth century over the issue of determinism, the view that every event has a cause. Are we caused to believe and to act, or are we free? Determinism paves the way for mechanistic and materialist views. Those who believe in free will, however, are much more likely to link freedom with an ability to reason, and perhaps both with morality. Certainly, extolling reason distinguished humans from the physical world in a significant way, and made them appear to be made in the image of God. Detachment from the cycle of physical processes gave them the opportunity to investigate and understand them. It was because humans were thought to be separated from the material world that the scientific investigation of matter became possible in the first place. The distinction between matter and spirit, between the physical world and our understanding, became of fundamental importance. It led to the dualism of the French philosopher, Descartes. He lived in the seventeenth century and, with his emphasis on the role of reason and his quest for philosophical certainty, is often thought to be the founder of modern philosophy. He made such a thorough separation of mind and matter that it became a major problem how the two could even interact within a human being. There was also the risk that, if mind or spirit were discarded, the only option left would be a thoroughgoing materialism. Certainly, unlike some of his contemporaries,

Descartes viewed the material world as devoid of spirit, and hence a mechanism. Yet as his epitaph in the ancient Paris church of Saint Germain-des-Prés stresses, he championed human reason, but left the authority of the Christian faith intact.

Science as a discipline could never have arisen without some idea that the scientist was different from the objects he was investigating. Reason could not be itself part of what was being investigated. It was the instrument of investigation and the precondition for it. One of those to exercise considerable influence in Cambridge, at the time of Newton, was Benjamin Whichcote, Provost of King's College during the Civil War, and still an influential figure in London after the restoration of the monarchy. He placed great emphasis on the role of human reason, perhaps because he was horrified by its absence in the turbulent times through which he lived. He placed it in a theological context, and for him reason was, in his favourite phrase, 'the candle of the Lord'. The phrase in fact became something of a slogan for the whole movement of so-called Cambridge Platonists. It was picked up later by John Locke, and epitomizes a view of reason which both extols it and also places it in the context of a belief in God. In other words, unlike later rationalism, such thinkers saw human reason as free and autonomous, but placed it in God's world and reflecting on God's creation. Reason was a candle giving the light of knowledge. Just as a candle gives a flickering and partial light, so the limitations, as well as the capacities, of human reason were recognized. Yet the gap between scientists and world is closed, in so far as it becomes less surprising that a God-given capacity for reason should be able to have grasped the way God has created the universe. It is thus not an accident that the physical world is intelligible to us. The human mind could understand something of the divine mind and its products, simply because the source of our understanding lies in God. With these beliefs, the conditions necessary for the growth of modern science were created. The European Enlightenment was born.

This example does not just show that modern science, as a matter of historical fact, happened to grow up within a theistic framework. A stress on human reason does not have to be motivated by materialism or atheism. Indeed, when science appears to be the only expression of that reason, and the reason is limited to what lies within the scope of science, the ensuing naturalism creates difficulties for the idea of rationality. We shall see how it is difficult to find room for any form of rationality in a mechanistic world. The science that establishes the mechanism poses questions about the conditions of its own possibility. The question is then how we can reason about the world, if reason is itself to be understood as part of a mechanistic process.

Autonomy and Choice

The idea of reason as the candle of the Lord is far removed from ideas current later in the Enlightenment. Human autonomy was to be celebrated by Kant, but the freedom connected with earlier ideas of reason was of a different kind. The logical outcome of a belief in autonomy was a refusal to accept that humans were constrained by the will of God in any sense. At the beginning of the Enlightenment, however, reason was not seen as opposed to God, but was made possible by Him, as guarantor of its validity. This did not involve the freedom of the artist facing a blank canvas. We are not free to create our world, or to decide what we shall find true. Later philosophers have stretched the role of human autonomy to the point where it appears that we have the freedom ourselves that a divine creator was supposed to have. Rational freedom in a theistic context is a freedom to recognize or reject the will of God. It is a freedom to come to understand or to neglect the glories of God's creation. It is a freedom to recognize a truth that is already there, to see a reality that already has a particular nature.

This type of freedom is also essential for the development of science. No science worthy of the name can flourish if the freedom of a scientist to be led to any conclusion is so unconstrained that a scientist can believe anything. Science is not a mere exercise of artistic freedom. Its freedom must be rational and conform to reality. Science has flourished under democratic regimes where there is a freedom to challenge and test ideas. Its conclusions should not be preordained by political necessity. The freedom to decide on areas of investigation is also important, so that scientific research is guided by the character of reality and not by ideology. No science would do well if theories are adopted merely because someone or some group wants them to be true.

Freedom is essential, but it must be contained within the ambit of rational investigation. It is not of an absolute kind. I am not free to decide that water is composed of nitrogen rather than hydrogen, or that atoms cannot be split. I can make mistakes, but I am not the source of what is real. The world may not make me believe something, but it will determine whether my belief is true. Science demands freedom, but it also depends on reasoning constrained by something beyond science. Only the real physical world can give science its purpose and goal. Some philosophers may find this freedom too limited, and certainly the extent of freedom in moral choice is controversial. Followers of Kant value human autonomy. They claim that we should be completely unconstrained by the nature of the world in deciding what is to count as good or right.

Once, however, freedom is viewed as being truly creative, the role of reason is diminished. It becomes merely an instrument, helping us to achieve the ends that we have set for ourselves. It can have no greater purpose, because when there is no external constraint on choice, there will be no reason for choosing one way rather than another. The choice is itself the ultimate, arbitrary fact. If I drive into a large, empty car park, with hundreds of marked spaces, there will be no reason to park in any particular space. I have to park somewhere, but it does not matter where. Choice becomes everything, and as a result becomes difficult. Reason is of little assistance, particularly if a large number of spaces are equidistant from the exit. Very few situations in life, however, are like this. Morality probably invokes a more rational process of thought than some people think. Science, however, certainly does. Our choices there are not arbitrary, but have to be measured against a world that possesses an inherent nature of its own. Science is not an exercise in expressing our own personality. It is an attempt to make discoveries.

One aspect of scientific reason, often stressed, is its alleged public character. This is one thing that attracted philosophers to the idea of verification. Religion can be accused of dabbling in mysteries that lie beyond our ability to recognize them. Alleged mystical experience cannot be shared. Morality is, it is said, a private matter. Only science deals with a form of reasoning that can be public property. Only science, it seems, is fit to walk on the public stage. All other alleged forms of reasoning are made to appear matters of private judgement, personal opinion, and subjective preference. Science can prove what it asserts, to the satisfaction of everyone. Scientific objectivity is often not so much connected with the objective character of the world as the public character of science. Evidence is of its nature inter-subjective, and can be shared, so it is argued. Private evidence, to which I alone have access, appears to be no evidence at all. This is why science can cut across cultural differences. Either something is regarded as being within the ambit of science, or it is relegated to the private sphere of the individual. This has certainly been the fate of religion, ethics and aesthetics. They have been regarded as the personal choice of the autonomous individual, and in the process have become regarded as not much more than a matter of taste.

Science has authority, but this may be as much a sociological fact as an epistemological one. In other words, people may happen to respect it for reasons which have little to do with questions of truth. Advertisers find that putting a figure in a white coat in order to make scientific pronouncements about, say, washing powder or toothpaste, can be effective. Scientists are seen as sources of authority in a way that clergy, for instance, no longer are. This is a social fact and could easily alter, given enough environmental problems arising from technological change, for example. The issue should not be whether scientists happen to be respected. The question is whether science should be pre-eminent, to the exclusion of other insights. It is a matter not just of what happens to be the case, but of what ought to be.

Science depends on reason, but once science becomes dominant it feels that it has to explain even our own processes of reason. This is crucially important in the present day. It is, however, an ancient programme. The Roman poet Lucretius, writing about Epicurean philosophy, said that everything was composed of atoms and void. He even considered that the human mind was very fine in texture, made of fine particles. Its behaviour is explicable in the same way as other parts of matter. Nearer to our present time, the Enlightenment may have extolled reason, but it soon produced materialists who wanted to root reason firmly in the material world, and not set it apart from it. Kant himself trod an uneasy path between a material world he saw as determined, and a rational world. Free judgements could be made in the latter by a self which is not imprisoned in matter. He drew a distinction between the 'phenomenal' world, the world as it appears to us, and the 'noumenal' world, that of pure reason. The problem remained of how the rational self could be properly located in a physical world.

Later philosophers, particularly in France, were under no doubt that humans are subordinate to physical laws. We are the mere result of combinations of matter. A French eighteenth-century materialist, Baron d'Holbach, says that 'matter alone is capable of acting on our senses, and without this action, nothing would be capable of making itself known to us'.[2] His argument is that we talk of spirit merely because of our ignorance of real causes. What is not matter can only be 'vacuum and emptiness'.[3] Needless to say, religion is one of his main targets (as it was for Lucretius). For him, God is seen as designating the unknown cause of whatever humans have either admired or dreaded. Talking of God, he thought, is really an expression of a lack of knowledge. In the same way, the idea of any immaterial substance is in fact an absence of ideas. It is a blank, a nothing, standing in for a something. There is more to this than anti-religious rhetoric. The point is that the world, namely everything that there is, is seen as a seamless and material whole. As d'Holbach asks: 'Is not nature herself a vast machine, of which the human species is but a very feeble spring?'⁴ The comparison with a machine is instructive, as machines are characteristically designed for purposes. That is not the main moral which a materialist would draw from the metaphor. Instead, the emphasis is on the material constitution of reality, and the fact that there is a closed system of causal laws. These would entail an absolute determinism. Human action is thus not free and neither is anything else. Humans are so embedded in the material world that no aspect of them can be thought distinct from it. Yet there is a question which all materialist philosophies must face: where does the proponent stand to be able to proclaim materialism? The belief and the proclamation are both themselves presumably to be understood as material parts of a material system. They are causally determined and not freely chosen. What part can human reason play in all this? Materialism may be the conclusion of a piece of human reasoning, but it is bound to change the way we see the scope and function of such reason.

There is a further problem. Determinism, at least in an earlier age, seemed to go easily with a materialist philosophy. If the world is a vast material machine, it will operate mechanistically, like any machine. The clockwork mechanism will be wound up, and the clock will perform its task in a predetermined way. It will strike, for instance, at the appropriate time. There is always the problem of who wound the clock up, and in the eighteenth century, God was given this residual role by so-called 'deists'. They strenuously resisted any idea that God could intervene in the law-governed universe. This undermined a broader theism, which saw God, in a more traditional way, as intervening more directly in human life. Yet once God had been relegated to the sidelines in this way, the next step was to dispense with God's services altogether. The world was then seen as a wholly determined machine built up solely of matter. Modes of explanation had no need to call on anything non-material, or to make the world depend on anything beyond itself. Theism slipped into deism, and deism paved the way for materialism. This seemed to many in the eighteenth century a welcome simplification. As well, however, as ruling out religion, this position made several vast philosophical assumptions. As we shall see, they are controversial even today.

Notes

1   *Theaetetus*, 174a.
2   Baron d'Holbach, *The System of Nature*, New York, 1808; reprinted by Lennox Hill (Burt Franklin), New York, 1970.
3   Ibid., p. 48.
4   Ibid., p. 112.

4

Modernity

Laws of Nature

The picture of the world as a vast machine with humans as part of its mechanism, or as 'a feeble spring', may have derived from the idea of a celestial craftsman who designed it all. In the eyes of the materialists, however, the machine existed in its own right, without any need for an explanation beyond itself. It functioned according to fixed laws which ensured that everything worked as it should. The idea of a law-giver may have been discarded, but the laws remained. Newtonian physics was able to describe the world in physical terms, without having to resort to the occult forces which had often been still invoked in the seventeenth century. Influences such as 'the spirit of nature', associating spiritual with physical processes, had often been called on. After Newton, it was recognized that even apparently mysterious forces, such as gravitation, could now be explained in physical terms. That set the agenda for the onward march of scientific understanding. Yet it was not just the role of God, the divine watchmaker, which was put into question. Attention was devoted to the nature of the mechanism. What was the position of 'the feeble spring', the human race? If the mechanism has been wound up, the various coils and springs are subject to the working of the other parts. The working is subject at every moment to a pattern of cause and effect. The whole is determined and its working is predictable. The various bits and pieces do not have any choice about how they perform, and clearly the moral to be drawn is that neither do we. We are just part of a similar mechanism on a larger scale.

We are not free agents and in fact, the materialists would claim, there is no mysterious part in humans which can initiate any free action. We are nothing more than our bodies, and are not separable in any way from them. D'Holbach says: 'To say that the soul shall feel, shall think, shall enjoy, shall suffer, after the death of the body, is to pretend that the clock, shivered into a thousand pieces, will continue to strike the hour, and have the faculty of marking the progress of time.'[1]

We are flesh and bone and have no invisible, intangible 'soul', it will be said, to be the subject of my choices and my reason. The self seemed to the materialists to be an illusion. Yet even so, they wished to uphold 'reason' and they talked of 'nature'. They still wished to refer to 'enlightenment' and 'demonstrating truth' in the pursuit of progress. At the same time as saying that truth is 'the only subject worthy the research of every wise man',[2] someone like d'Holbach could claim 'man is the work of nature and subject to her laws, from which he cannot free himself, nor even exceed in thought'.[3]

Reason and truth were thought compatible with a rigid determinism, and materialism. Indeed, the belief in uniform and invariable laws gave ground to an expectation that the world was intelligible and meaningful. It was not a conglomeration of arbitrary chaos. The law-giver had been dethroned, but it was still taken for granted that the world was orderly and regular in its behaviour. It had its own inherent rationality and was predictable, even though the divine source for that reason had been jettisoned. The uniformity of nature justified the pursuit of science, but had itself lost any grounding or rationale. Nature was uniform, and that was that. Some more reflective philosophers could appeal to our experience and give a justification in terms of the fact that our experience shows this to be so. This, though, merely raises again the venerable problem of induction, concerning how we can predict future experience on the basis of what is past.

It was assumed that physical laws were sufficient to explain the behaviour of physical objects. Causal explanation, through the invocation of such laws, became the only form of permissible explanation. Knowledge of how the clock worked was enough, and there was no need to invoke the intentions of the clockmaker. Although, too, the cautious empiricist would think of laws in terms of summaries of our experience, it was very easy for them to be seen as having a more directive role. The very analogy with laws of the land suggests that we are not just talking about what happens to occur. We are talking of what is supposed to take place. Laws about, say, speed limits on roads, do not summarize the average speed motorists reach along a stretch of motorway. They lay down what is regarded as a safe maximum speed. It is no defence for driving at ninety miles an hour that a significant number of other cars were doing so as well. If you, yourself, were still breaking the law, you could be punished. In other words, laws typically prescribe, rather than describe. They attempt to set standards and influence behaviour. The very fact a law is passed by a legislature should have an effect on how people behave.

Yet problems arise if this is used as an analogy for the laws of nature, particularly as they have been regarded since the eighteenth century. We have already seen that the picture of laws becomes awkward without a law-giver or legislature. Self-generated laws of nature can mean little more than tendencies within physical systems to operate in a certain fashion. It seems hard to envisage the laws existing somehow apart from physical behaviour. This conception of law as prescribing the behaviour of physical objects distinct from them is a profoundly anti-materialist view. It has its roots in a Platonic idea of some realm of eternal standards, existing necessarily, of which this physical world is a pale copy. Laws are very abstract entities and cannot be allowed any proper explanatory role in a materialist system. By definition, they cannot exist apart from the events of which they are instances. That, however, means that when we refer to such laws, we must, at least according to a consistent materialist, merely describe what tends to happen.

A view of laws as physical tendencies in the world is far from a conception of an iron-bound necessity, of laws determining, or prescribing, events. It is not the same as imagining that things have to happen because of some extraneous constraint. Without God, and without the idea of anything existing apart from physical processes themselves, all reason can do is to describe and correlate. Yet, as we have seen, reason itself cannot be detached from the ongoing march of physical events. According to a strong materialist, and determinist position, human rationality is part of the material world and cannot somehow be abstracted from it. This produces an unbearable tension.

A mechanistic view of laws of nature operating in a closed system produces its own contradictions. In the eighteenth century, opponents of religion could subtract God and the human mind from the picture and think that everything else could stay the same. In essence, they wanted to study the watch while denying the existence of a watchmaker. Yet how can we be any longer certain that scientists are studying an analogue of a watch?

Mechanisms and Machines

Talk of laws and mechanisms inevitably invokes some ideas of purposive creation and design. A belief in a strict determinism, of event regularly following cause, and in its turn producing pre-ordained effects, suggests an ordered universe with its own structure. We certainly could not survive as a biological species in a sea of disorder. Yet determinism has been a metaphysical doctrine, since its assertion must always involve claims about physical events beyond our knowledge. It is talking about all physical processes everywhere and not just the ones that we can experience. Such global claims have to be metaphysical, since they could never be arrived at through science. Whatever irregularities are discovered scientifically, it is always possible that we then come to a brick wall and find ourselves unable to discover more. We can, of course, as with naturalism, adopt a methodological presupposition and assume determinism as part of a methodology. We look for causes and take it for granted that they are there even if we cannot find any. That may be a good way of achieving progress in science, but we may still find that we are looking for something that does not exist. There are, in fact, several examples in modern physics, where there has been controversy over precisely where there are hidden causes. The question is whether we are unable to uncover them, or whether there is an intrinsic indeterminism in reality.

The most obvious example is that of quantum mechanics. The behaviour of sub-atomic particles seems radically different on occasion from that of the objects dealt with by the classical physics of Newton. There appears to be an inherent unpredictability in their individual behaviour. This is smoothed out so that there is a statistical regularity in the collective behaviour of particles. One may not be able to predict the behaviour of a particular particle, but overall one can be sure of their general behaviour. This accounts for the stability of the familiar world around us. Chaos theory provides another example of unpredictability. Minute changes in initial conditions, too small to be detectable, can be amplified into major results. The hackneyed example is that the flap of a butterfly's wings on one side of the world can produce perturbations which eventually result in a hurricane on the other. Yet unlike quantum events, this is much easier to see as consistent with determinism. What chaos theory shows is not that events are undetermined, but that there are limitations on our ability to predict them. It is a warning of too easily assimilating the fact of causation with what we, as humans, can predict. Not everything that is determined need be predictable. This is another example of how what is real should not be equated with any human ability to find it out.

The indeterminacy referred to by quantum mechanics demonstrates that contemporary physics does not assume the truth of metaphysical determinism. Einstein hankered after 'hidden variables' to explain quantum phenomena. He ran the risk of confusing the need to talk of a determinate, objective reality, with the need to hold on to the determinism of classical physics. There is no contradiction in assuming that there is an objective, physical reality, but that some of its processes are intrinsically undetermined, and even random. The world is not a mechanism, like a clock, according to contemporary science. It is much more fluid than that. In other words, talk of clocks or watches and their makers is beside the point. There is no watch. The world is not a mechanism. At the very least, the eighteenth-century view of matter was far too simple.

Yet, it may be asked, are we not using science (in this case, modern physics) to prove a philosophical point? Having said that determinism is a metaphysical thesis, are we not now saying that it has been shown to be mistaken by physics? In other words, empirical science seems to have intervened. This is the reverse of the actual situation. Arguments about the interpretation of quantum mechanics show how our philosophy is not so much the handmaiden of science as its foundation. The ability of quantum mechanics to manipulate the physical world is not in question. Arguments never centre on what it can do, but rather on what it all means. Do microscopic particles exist in their own right, and what is their nature? How do they affect each other? Can there be any action between them from a distance? Basic issues surface about the nature of reality and of causation; the responses we give are formed by our philosophical views.

Positivists who believe in the importance of verification will place great emphasis on the role of instruments measuring microscopic phenomena. They will refuse to countenance the independent reality of particles, just because they are unobservable. At most, positing them will prove useful shorthand, they think, for the prediction of future observations. Similarly, idealists, who want to stress the supremacy of the human mind, will claim that quantum phenomena have no reality until they register on human consciousness through instruments. A realist, on the other hand, may assume the objective reality of sub-atomic processes, but then have to accept that they may be very different in kind from those of ordinary objects dealt with in classical physics. Indeterminacy may be part of their nature.

Arguments about the right way to understand quantum mechanics, and how its mathematical formalism applies to the physical world, do not settle philosophical disputes. They are themselves a reflection of those disputes. Science cannot settle philosophical questions. The sense we give to scientific discoveries, and the way in which they are described, is itself the result of a prior philosophical understanding. Nowhere is this more true than in the way we envisage scientific laws, and use machines and mechanisms as appropriate metaphors for the working of reality in general and the human mind in particular.

We have already remarked that machines generally imply the presence of design and purpose. Indeed, the comparison between the workings of the world and those of a watch enabled a popular argument from design to the existence of God to be given currency in the nineteenth century. If we find a watch, it is of course reasonable to assume that it has been specifically designed. The problem with the physical world is, however, whether the comparison with a watch is reasonable in the first place. The assimilation to the idea of mechanism already imports ideas of order and function. They, in turn, raise the question of whose purposes are being worked out. The problem is not so much whether there is a divine watchmaker, but whether we are confronted with, or live in, something that is like a watch in the first place. Machines are typically the result of a causal process. They have been made or programmed. Their purpose and function is given them from outside. Machines do not need to have any understanding of what they are doing. Indeed, the problem of comparing humans with feeble springs is precisely that springs act and react automatically. They do not need to have any comprehension themselves of what is happening, or how they are behaving. Mechanisms typically cannot exercise any judgement, have any reasons or have any opportunity to exercise creativity. They are not free. Some materialist philosophers, like Hobbes in the seventeenth century, tried to say that freedom is mere lack of constraint. A machine is thereby free, merely because its parts are moving freely because they are unobstructed. This is a very attenuated sense of freedom. Arguments over whether people have free will, or are caused to act through a combination of genetic and environmental influences on them, are not settled by pointing out that we can move our bodies because we are not tied up.

Machines have their goals presented to them and cannot change their views on what is worth pursuing. As machines become more sophisticated and we enter the world of computing, philosophical distinctions between mechanical and purposive action become more difficult to draw. Clocks are relatively simple mechanisms. Thermostats react to the environment and can produce effects, such as turning central heating on, as a result of a change in temperature. Self-guiding missiles and other machines with feedback mechanisms are more complicated. Nevertheless, in all these cases, there is still an apparent distinction between the causal behaviour of the machine and the rational intentions of the designer. It is the purpose of the materialist, and the naturalist, in philosophy to insist that there is never a fundamental distinction between human artefacts and the humans themselves. The fault, they would say, in the comparison between humans and feeble springs, did not lie in the idea of comparing us with a part of physical reality. The whole point, they would say, is that we are ourselves part of physical reality. Yet, despite our undoubted complexity, we are being compared with a simple artefact. Human beings are vastly more able to achieve things than bits of a watch. Materialists would claim that, in spite of this, we are ourselves wholly material.

There is a touching tendency among materialists in any age to wish to invoke the most impressive artefacts of their time, and say that humans are not really different from them. At the beginning of the twenty-first century the comparison is with computers. A naturalist is always bound to assume that humans are replicable by computers. Human reason will appear no different in principle from the processes which a computer can and will be programmed to perform. This means that any explanation of agency has in the end to be a causal one. Mechanistic views, however sophisticated, have to interpret events in terms of cause and effect, rather than reason and purpose. Whether or not these two distinct sets of terms are in fact radically different is a major philosophical issue, to which we shall return.

The Reaction against Modernity

Whatever materialist tendencies surfaced during the Enlightenment, the allegiance to reason remained unshakeable. There was a time-bomb ticking here, as it is far from clear how far rationality and materialism are compatible. For the moment, however, 'Reason' had supplanted God. Human rationality was thought capable of grasping truth for itself. Tradition was decried as the repository of superstition, and the authority was thought to reside in reason rather than in the Sovereign or the Church. The extolling of human reason led to the downgrading of the idea of reality. The emphasis changed from what the world is like to how we experience or describe the world. This was epitomized by Kant's 'Copernican revolution'.

Kant drew a parallel between his own philosophy and the theories of Copernicus. Just as the latter showed that the spectator revolves around the stars rather than, as might appear, the reverse, so all reality is structured by the concepts of rational beings. According to Kant, reason does not follow the nature of reality. We may easily assume that we are at rest and the heavens revolving. In the same way, we might think that concepts such as those of space, time or cause, reflect the way things are. Kant, however, maintained that such concepts give us the conditions under which we can structure the world. He thought that they are about us, rather than simply about a reality which, anyway, could not be seen as it was in itself. Kant's work stimulated a belief in the importance of 'categorial frameworks', the assumptions which we bring to bear on our experience. The focus was on the human perspective rather than on what is seen through the perspective. Reason became a feature of human beings rather than a link with reality. Reality, for Kant, was the world as it was in itself, totally independent of the way it appeared to anyone. Once appearances were invoked they had to be structured and influenced by the way we thought and by the concepts we had at our disposal. Reality, as a result, receded into the distance and became an inaccessible something, which could only be viewed through the possibly distorting lens of our own categories.

A Kantian approach sits uneasily with the materialist approach to the world, even though both have their roots in the same Enlightenment ideal of universal reason. For the materialist, reason reflects nature and its laws. Indeed, it has to be part of the natural process and subject to its laws. Kant and his followers wanted to abstract reason from what they saw as the phenomenal world. Reason is then separate and free. Yet this opposition to naturalism brings with it definite anthropocentric tendencies. The focus shifts from the real world to rational beings in general, and to humans in particular. We no longer find ourselves concerned with the nature of the world. Instead, in humanist fashion, we start with humans and their reactions to the 'world'. Our perspectives, our interpretations and our understanding become of primary importance.

Anyone who wants to be both a humanist and a materialist will often find that the two viewpoints start pulling in opposite directions. The urge to see humans as special militates against the idea that we are just lumps of stuff, even intricate ones like clocks or computers. The stress on human judgement begins to pull us apart from any idea that we are in touch with the real world. Both viewpoints are opposed to any idea of God, and this betrays their origins in the Enlightenment, at least in some of its manifestations. For the materialist, the physical world by definition replaces any spiritual one. The stress on human reason explicitly challenges any notion of what is sometimes called in present-day philosophy, 'a God's-eye view'. There is thought to be no absolute viewpoint from which reality even in principle can be seen. Everything is then conditioned by the facts of who we are and where we are. Our own perspective colours everything.

All this has led to an increasing hostility to what is currently regarded as the classical Enlightenment view of reason. Any rational claim to universal truth has been challenged over the closing decades of the twentieth century. 'Modernity' has in fact been superseded in some quarters by so-called 'postmodernism'. This has involved a conscious reaction against the all-encompassing claims of Enlightenment rationality. They were seen as claiming truth for everyone everywhere. Instead, the significance of tradition and its influence on our reasoning has been stressed. Just as Kuhn saw that science itself is built on its own traditions, seen as 'paradigms', so greater emphasis has been given to the different perspectives arising from different traditions. No longer is reason supreme, but it is regarded as having grown out of local conditions, which may vary from place to place and time to time. Above all, reason is seen as rooted in various historical contexts. The place of history, and historical development, is said to be crucial. The idea of abstracting oneself from one's own historical condition and conducting a rational debate with great thinkers of different epochs is viewed with great suspicion. The thought that we can argue about Plato's theories as if we were his own contemporaries is laughed at. Ideas and opinions, it is suggested, grow out of their own historical context and can never be properly understood when torn apart from it. Our own understanding must be the product of our own age and cannot be removed from its own context, which gives it its life.

How then do we understand historical texts? How can we interpret what people of an earlier age thought? Attacks on the idea of an overarching, ahistorical rationality suggest that we cannot. We can read and interpret texts, but the reading is ours and we are likely to bring as much to the text, through the presuppositions of our own age, as we extract from it. Indeed, it seems that all interpretations have to be governed by a context and location. There must be some truth in all this. A theatrical production of, say, Shakespeare, always bears the imprint of its own age. A historical novel very often reveals as much about the time it was written, as the time it purports to be about. It is remarkably easy for authors to produce fiction in which the characters behave like their own acquaintances. A book written about the

England of the 1930s will be significantly different if it was actually written at that time, rather than the present day.

The Lure of Pragmatism

Distrust in the possibility of a detached rationality reached its logical conclusion in thinking of the Enlightenment view of reason as itself one tradition among many. Indeed, there were apparently several Enlightenment ideas of reason, ranging from the religious views of reason as reflecting the rationality, or 'logos', of God, to secular, and even materialist, versions. A contemporary American philosopher, Richard Rorty, says bluntly that 'I see the Western Rationalist Tradition as a secularized version of the Western Monotheistic Tradition'.[4] In other words, God became transmuted into Reason. Yet when Reason itself is seen in a more concrete or historicized fashion it may seem less impersonal and imperious. It is reduced to the actual reasoning of particular people. We are then, however, only left with the fact of conflicting opinions, within and between societies. What, it may be said, has happened to the notions of truth and reality? As long as reason was seen as our guide, these could be our goals. As Rorty, however, points out, the secularism of the later Enlightenment removed any supernatural grounding for our rationality. It took great delight in the fact that humans are on their own. Human autonomy became an end in itself and was totally unconstrained. Humans had, in Rorty's words, 'no supernatural light to guide them to the Truth.' He continues: 'But of course the Enlightenment replaced the idea of such guidance with the idea of a quasi-divine faculty called "reason". It is this idea which American pragmatists, and post-Nietzschean European philosophers, are attacking.'[5]

Rorty sees himself as an American pragmatist, more interested in agreement than truth, in 'conversation' than metaphysics, in what is within our reach rather than what is beyond it. Pragmatists are impatient with distinctions that can make no practical difference. Although pragmatism is undoubtedly a subtle philosophy itself, it can be seen to challenge the whole practice of philosophy. It asks why we should waste time arguing about truth if it makes no difference to our lives here and now. The essential question, it may seem, will not be 'is it true?', but 'what difference does it make to our lives?' Once abstract reasoning is challenged, so is the possibility of any access to truth or reality. What comes to matter is the fact of our belief, and not what our beliefs may or may not be about. It seems to be important how we get on with others on our society, and whether we can agree, but not whether that agreement is about 'Truth'.

An example of this approach comes from a story once told by William James, a famous American pragmatist philosopher of the nineteenth century.[6] He recounts how, when on a trip in upstate New York with friends, he went for a walk and came back to find a fierce argument in progress. They had seen a squirrel and, as squirrels do, it tried to go round the back of the trunk of a tree to keep away from them. They went round the tree to catch up with it and, as they did so, it also went round the tree to stay away from them. So it went on. The problem they were arguing about was simply whether they were going round the squirrel. James felt that this was a good example of all the faults of a metaphysical argument. Nothing hung on it, and it made no practical difference what one said. In fact, it all depended on what was meant by 'going round'. Without a practical difference between alternatives, there could be no real difference in meaning. Even if one maintained that truth was at stake, it was not a truth that influenced anything. Metaphysical questions, in other words, must be vacuous, unless they could have a discernible effect on human practice. Otherwise, James claims, dispute is idle.

Pragmatists are inclined to look at the concrete, rather than the abstract, and to despise lofty impersonal notions like 'reason' or 'truth'. Their concern is with people and the circumstances in which they make their judgements, rather than with what, if anything, the judgements are about. Typical is Rorty's view that 'we should move from claims to knowledge and self-evidence to suggestions what we should try'.[7] He attacks the idea that the prime purpose of language is to be about reality. He says that we should instead start thinking of words 'as nodes in the causal network which binds the organism together with its environment.'[8] We suddenly seem to be back with something like the machine metaphor. It appears that we are linked causally to our environment.

What has happened? Rorty, like many, has adopted a postmodernist attack on ideas of reason. This must result in his having to distance himself from the very notion of scientific reasoning, which was one of the great legacies of the Enlightenment. One possible result of this is to see science as one body of belief, which is no better or worse than any other. Wittgenstein was probably the most influential philosopher of the twentieth century, at least in the English-speaking world. He was an Austrian, who worked with Bertrand Russell, the Cambridge logician, and so his work is the outcome of numerous influences. He started off by seeing words as labels for things, naming them, but in his later philosophy he saw them much more as tools. The meaning of a word lay in the way it was used. This is much nearer the pragmatist approach, rooting words in ways of life, rather than letting them be pawns in some abstruse and metaphysical game. Yet this will always raise the question why a word should be used in one way rather than another. Why should we be attached to one way of life rather than another? What is the point of, say, scientific language? In fact, Wittgenstein found it very difficult in some of his latest work, just before he died in 1951, to justify attachment to physics rather in the belief in anything else, such as oracles. It was all like playing a game, an analogy which he liked, referring to 'language-games'. If you play a game, there are clear rules and you know what you ought to be doing. There is, though, no ultimate reason for playing one game rather than another. One soccer manager was once accused of taking his game too seriously and treating it like a religion. His answer was that soccer was much more important than that. Yet we know that this is a joke, because games are games, even when played for vast amounts of money. Religion, on the other hand, has to claim truth, or it is nothing. Wittgenstein, and indeed pragmatists, are in danger of obliterating a distinction like this. Games, astrology, oracles, science and religion are then all human practices, and have to be accepted on an equal footing.

While pragmatism is tempted to treat all human practices equally, it also wants to give priority to science. At times, it seems to want to make science the sole source of knowledge. We have already seen how Rorty is happy to talk in causal terms, and he is also ready to accept the label of 'naturalist'. He wants to break down distinctions between science and philosophy in the familiar way which makes philosophy follow in the wake of scientific understanding. As he says, 'the American pragmatist tradition . . . has made a point of breaking down the distinctions between philosophy, science, and politics'.[9] The merging of philosophy and science is always part of the naturalist programme because it despises metaphysics and the idea of any metaphysical grounding for science. We then have to accept scientific practices at their face value. The addition of politics is significant, since it makes explicit the pragmatist view that truth is a meaningless abstraction when prised apart from agreement. The crucial point for a pragmatist of Rorty's ilk would be to obtain agreement, and not use reason as a guide to truth or to a knowledge of reality. Truth is then about what people accept and come to believe. It is a construction out of people's attitudes, and not an objective goal in some metaphysical realm. Rorty is explicitly opposed to any form of Platonic dualism, whether between this world and another, time and eternity, mind and spirit, belief and knowledge, or agreement and truth. All such distinctions involve prising our life here on earth apart from something else, which may seem inaccessible and irrelevant. Rorty himself understands the wider significance of what he is saying. He claims that 'when Platonic dualisms go, the distinction between philosophy and the rest of culture is in danger'.[10]

Philosophy at the present day faces two conflicting temptations. It can be overcome with the success of science and accept that philosophy on its own can discover nothing and understand nothing. Its task is to clarify and systematize the findings of science. That is the naturalist programme, and to a large extent it follows in the footsteps of the mechanistic and materialist views of early generations. The difference is that it has developed into a much more sophisticated position with the onward march of contemporary science. On the other hand, philosophy can be seduced by the postmodernist attacks on the possibility of reason. It can come to accept that human reason is always historically situated, and is never unbiased or unprejudiced. All cultural developments thus involve clashes between beliefs and attitudes, which can never be finally resolved in a rational way. We then have no choice but to live in pluralist societies which are not based on one set of principles, but include instead varying practices and beliefs. There is no way of achieving agreement, other than a resort to threats and violence. Pluralism, the toleration of alternative ways of life, can seem the only peaceful outcome. Another consequence is that, with the demolition of reason, philosophy itself is left with nowhere to stand. A philosophy that is tied down to the attitudes of a particular culture becomes a mere fact about that culture. In so far as it reflects on and talks about the background which produced it, it begins to look more like mere cultural commentary rather than genuine philosophical understanding. As we have seen, rational criticism is impossible without an element of detachment. In other words, it involves the kind of rationality which postmodernism says is impossible.

Thus, on the one hand, a naturalist philosophy becomes absorbed into science. The latter is left with no possibility of justification, other than the mere fact that the Western world, and in fact the whole world, happens at the moment to practise it. On the other hand, postmodernist philosophy becomes submerged in the cultural currents of the day. Both threaten the future of philosophical thinking, one from an Enlightenment perspective, glorifying the sciences, and the other from a reaction against the Enlightenment. Yet the curious fact is that some people, such as Richard Rorty, want to ride both horses at once. They decry reason and want to break down the distinction between philosophy and the rest of culture. At the same time, they do not wish to give up their respect for science. They seem to believe that people ought to accept the methods and findings of science, and certainly take comfort in the cultural fact that science still retains its hegemony in the Western world. Instead of epistemology and metaphysics, Rorty prefers what he terms 'cultural politics'.[11] Instead of claims to knowledge, he prefers to offer suggestions about what we should try. Why, though, should we try anything? Pragmatists like to talk of what is useful, instead of what is true. Nevertheless, claims about what is and is not useful still appear to be claims about what is true. Hoping that something will be useful does not make it so. The mere existence of a practice does not of itself prove that the practice is worthwhile or beneficial. No practice, not even physics, can be accepted at face value. If the suggestion is that we do so because there are physicists, we have to face the question why we should not also accept astrology. There are self-proclaimed astrologers, as daily newspapers bear witness. They have an enthusiastic readership even in a scientific age. Are we to say that if people have beliefs, that is enough to justify them? The problem of relativism beckons.

Notes

1 Baron d'Holbach, *The System of Nature*, New York, 1808; reprinted by Lennox Hill (Burt Franklin), New York, 1970, p. 119.
2 Ibid., p. 330.
3 Ibid., p. 340.
4 Richard Rorty, *Truth and Progress, Philosophical Papers 3*, Cambridge University Press, Cambridge, 1998, p. 76.
5 Richard Rorty, *Philosophy and Social Hope*, Penguin Books, Harmondsworth, 1999, p. xxvii.
6 *The Work of William James: Pragmatism*, Harvard University Press, Cambridge, MA, 1975, pp. 27–8.
7 *Philosophy and Social Hope*, p. 57.
8 Ibid., p. xxiii.
9 Ibid., p. xx.
10 Ibid.
11 *Truth and Progress*, p. 57.

5

Relativism and its Flaws

Tradition and Truth

Enlightenment thinkers wished to appeal to public reason, which could settle all disputes, regardless of their origin. For them, tradition was an impedi-
ment, and authority a threat. Once reason was freed of such obstacles it
could make a universal appeal, and all our problems, quite literally, would be
over. Human progress would be assured. Things have not worked out like
that in the intervening years. Instead, the postmodern reaction to such views
has reinstated tradition. The problem, though, is that there is never just one
tradition, but a multiplicity. We are each in fact the product of many inter-
locking traditions. Our 'culture' is a result of many influences, just as it is
often far from clear who 'we' are. Even in an area as small as Great Britain,
there is often debate as to whether people are primarily British, or English,
Scottish or Welsh. Matters become even more fraught across the Irish Sea in
Northern Ireland. There the labels 'British' or 'Irish' draw attention to deep
divisions in what can scarcely be called a single community. Some Northern
Irish refuse to be called 'British', whilst others consider that is precisely what
they are. Even above all this, there are further disputes about how far the
British are to be considered, first and foremost, Europeans.

Divisions of different kinds can be quickly uncovered in most countries.
The United States of America is often called 'a pluralist society', and it is
apparent that it is made up of many traditions and cultures, not to mention
languages. One cannot always predict from the mere knowledge that someone is American what beliefs or customs will be held. Common allegiance to
a political system, which is itself tolerant of diversity, is about all one could

hope for. Yet it is not a matter of different, self-contained traditions existing alongside each other. We are all influenced by each other, wherever we are. Traditions are not watertight compartments. They are, in fact, very porous, able to soak up many varying influences. The more that 'tradition' is emphasized, the less clear it often is what is being appealed to. I can categorize myself by highlighting differences from other people. I could then find that my 'community' is so specialized that it has a membership of one.

The less notice taken of truth and reality, the more the fact of different beliefs will be stressed. They might then seem true only for the group which expresses them. Yet if we cannot appeal to societies, or cultures, it becomes very difficult to identify groups. No doubt there was a time, when explorers first visited geographically separate tribes on, say, a Pacific island, in which it made sense to talk of separate communities and societies. When, however, near-naked New Guinea tribesmen can be photographed watching satellite television, it is obvious, even in 'remote' areas, that cultural boundaries are becoming blurred.

Whilst, therefore, the postmodernist attack on public reason has seemed to rehabilitate traditions and encourage a pluralist approach, it is far from clear how traditions are to be clearly identified. Does the fact of fundamental disagreement between groups of people indicate a divergence of tradition? This is a process which can be continued indefinitely, to the point where my own disagreements with others isolate me in my own personal tradition. One can see this process occurring when people are classified in groups, so that racial origin, sexual orientation, disability or lack of it, religious belief, gender, age, and so on, and so on, are all thought relevant to deciding which social grouping someone belongs to. Yet if one does not go down what looks like a rather ridiculous path, it will be very difficult to describe just which group certain beliefs are relative to. If one just talks of Western civilization, or of being British or American, we explain very little because the group appealed to may encompass tremendous differences in belief. There will be very few beliefs that are held by the whole of the group.

One problem is that groups sometimes define themselves into existence. Perhaps, indeed, the logical conclusion of any relativist position is that if you think a particular group exists, it does. If you think you are a member, you are. Yet a belief in relativism is a belief that beliefs are true for those who hold them. They are not true for everyone, let alone objectively or absolutely true. It follows that it may be true for me that I am a member of a special group, but I cannot expect it to be true for anybody else, if they choose not to believe it. Truth is a consequence of belief for relativism, and is restricted to those who hold the belief. I cannot expect that whatever I believe is true for anyone else, when they do not share my beliefs.

This argument can be generalized. Those who accept the truth of relativism may find it obvious that beliefs are not true for those who do not hold them. Yet this means that their own belief in relativism cannot hold for other people. Relativism may be true for some, but it cannot be true for its opponents. There does seem to be something very odd about this. If I believe that truth is relative, and that there is no such thing as objective truth, am I not making a claim about the nature of truth? I am surely doing more than reiterating my own belief if I assert that anything is true. Indeed, belief, like asserting anything in a language, is intimately linked with truth as its goal. Not all beliefs are true by a long way, and not everything that people say is true. If, however, we subtract the idea of truth from both belief and the use of language, how can we any longer have a belief that something is the case, or make assertions about it in a language? Communicating with other people typically involves invoking reference to a shared world. Claims to truth, as the Enlightenment stressed, involve claims which demand universal acceptance. That does not mean that they will be accepted universally. There is no belief so daft that someone somewhere is not prepared to hold it. Even the firmest findings of contemporary science do not command universal recognition. For one thing, not everyone can understand their significance. For another, no piece of evidence is so compelling that it cannot be rejected. It may be irrational to do so, but that is not the point. People can be, and are, irrational. It is still possible for them to believe that the earth is flat, even when they are presented with photographs from space which prove the contrary. They can say that the photographs have been produced as result of a subtle conspiracy.

In other words we must once again distinguish between the nature of the world and people's beliefs. Language attempts to refer to the world as it is and assumes we all normally have access to the same world. Truth and falsity are reflected in the success or failure of language to do this. Yet this is what relativism has to deny. It can only see what beliefs are held and what agreements or conventions arise. It loses any conception of a world beyond our beliefs. When disagreements are pronounced, and societies no longer homogeneous, it is possible (as it was for many Athenians at the time of Socrates) to become obsessed with this fact. Truth seems merely a by-product of belief and assertion, rather than their goal. Yet this must mean that there is no constraint on what is believed, apart from convention and the norms of a society. When societies no longer have sharp boundaries, there seems little point in believing one thing rather than another. My first thoughts are as likely to be right as my last, because it seems that there is no distinction between 'being right' and having a belief. The path to nihilism, where nothing seems to matter and no view is preferable to any other, beckons. There seems little point in believing anything if I can believe anything with impunity, without any idea of being constrained by the real world.

A Shared World

Truth is the indispensable presupposition of all thought and language, otherwise anything goes. All thought and all statements become as good as each other. As Plato argued in the *Theaetetus*, when language is no longer understood as being about a stable, shared world, all distinctions break down. He was arguing against Heraclitus' idea of a world in a state of constant change, but he also had Protagorean relativism in mind. Varying judgements made at different moments may be equally right, if the world is constantly changing. A dog for me may be a cat to you and a pile of bricks to someone else. This may seem ludicrous, but we need to grasp the idea of a world where dogs stay as dogs and cats as cats, or do so for a sufficient length of time for us to be able to draw each other's attention to them. Unless this is so, you can never understand what I mean by 'dog', because every time I point at something, and you look at it, it will have changed. Indeed, this point is even more fundamental. Language could never be taught in the first place without the assumption of a shared world. This must imply an element of stability. A little child looking at an animal must be presumed to see what its parent is seeing. When told that it is a dog, the child can then learn the word and gradually understand how to identify new examples of dogs. This process of elementary communication becomes impossible if my world is not my child's. We must assume the existence of a shared world and realize that we all normally have access in the same way to it. This will not always be the case. A blind child would not be able to learn the word 'dog' in the same way as a sighted one. Touch, for instance, may become more important, but even here the learning of language will depend on the assumption that there is a shared object which both parent and child can experience in the same way.

Once a relativist uses language to claim relativism, a series of assumptions come into play which must undermine the claim. The very existence of language, and the fact that it has been taught and learnt, suggest a shared world independent of the language. The assertion of relativism itself invokes the normal truth-stating functions of language. The idea that it is true that there is no such thing as truth is a seductive one, but it should be obvious that it is flagrantly self-contradictory. The mere act of asserting the truth of relativism to other people is self-destructive. There is no point in saying anything if relativism is true, because one then cannot claim truth through language.

Some may feel that this argument is still too slick. It is all very well, they might claim, showing how truth is a goal. The corollary may seem to be that, without that goal, thought and speech become as pointless and random as the behaviour of a group of would-be footballers milling about on a piece of grass, without any goals marked out, or even any agreed directions to play in. There is a difference between kicking a football around with others and playing a game with rules. The latter has a purpose and depends on agreement about what counts as winning. What, though, if there are different games with different rules, like, say, soccer and rugby? What counts as a goal is different in each case. Might there not be different conventions which have alternative views of truth? Truth as a goal may be indispensable, but what if there are different truths?

It may be recognized that there is a difficulty about drawing sharp distinctions between societies, or deciding what is to count as one game rather than another. This does not alter the fact, it may be claimed, that, in principle, there may be different conventions in different societies. Reference to language itself may be all very well, but we all know that there are many different languages. Perhaps each language itself demands shared assumptions, but why, it might be asked, should they all make the same assumptions? In this kind of discussion it has often been pointed out how the words of one language may often not have equivalents in another. The German word 'angst', with reference to an emotional state, and the Welsh 'hwyl', with reference to a style of preaching, have no simple equivalents in English. The argument against relativism may have shown that languages need shared rules and agreement between speakers in their basic judgements. Does that of itself prove the need for one, objective world, confronting everyone?

The later Wittgenstein, indeed, made much of the necessity of agreement and rules as a basis for communication, in his 'language-games'. He is himself often accused of a linguistic idealism, and even relativism, which refuses to see that language is about anything that can be identified independently of language. Yet if we only have access to the world through language, and identify bits of it by means of language, how can we talk of a world apart from language? We might think that such a world underpins the language and justifies its use, but this could merely be begging the question. It assumes the falsity of relativism in providing arguments against it. It assumes that the world comes in precisely the ready-packaged parcels that our language appears to give us. Another image would hold that it is assuming that language is carving nature at the joints. In other words, language gives us the distinctions that nature has already delineated.

Those who stress the priority of language over thought would deny this. Language gives us our distinctions, they hold. It creates them and does not discover them. Yet if that is the case, may we still not make a case for relativism, but this time relative to a language? Certain distinctions are true for one language, but not another; certain things can be said in one and not another. In other words, perhaps our agreements are not the result of some arbitrary social groupings, or chance agreement, but rather arise out of the language we are taught to speak. Different languages, particularly those unrelated to each other historically, may therefore create radically different worlds.

Some empirical data may apparently support this. A favourite example is the way in which languages may not all distinguish colour in the same way. Some take note of differences in shading that others ignore. Homer talks of a 'wine-dark' sea and nobody is quite sure whether he is talking of the colour itself or the depth of the hue. Might some ancient wine have been deep blue? Not all languages are the same, and translation is not always easy. Yet translation between human languages not only does take place, but we all assume that it can. What makes this assumption possible? If we were all locked up in the different worlds created by our respective languages, switching from one world to another would be difficult enough. Translation demands much more than this. A proper translation requires a correlation between the parts of one language with those of another. This cannot just happen. There must be some underlying rationale to make it a proper and feasible undertaking.

What sense can a relativist make of translation? The idea of one objective world, to which we all can appeal, may be given up. Even then, some correlation must be found between the circumstances in which one bit of language is uttered and those in which an apparently equivalent bit of another is. How can a relativist step out of one world to survey another and make connections between them? If all truth is relative to a particular language, we cannot even identify other languages, or the practices within which they are embedded, except through the medium of our own. In other words, we can never step outside our own language or even see the possibility of alternative distinctions being made. To begin translating, even a relativist has to assume that languages can be correlated and similarities identified. Yet this is not dependent on a judgement for a particular point of view. We have to assume some way of building bridges between languages. If, further, a bridge is a mere invention of one's own language, it is not really a bridge. It would be like a real bridge over an estuary, which is only supported on one side, and therefore never reaches the other.

Translation and Conceptual Differences

Some would-be relativists take the fact of translation for granted, but they ought not to. There must always be a question of how it can be justified. It is a project fraught with difficulties and the possibility of misunderstanding. Indeed some misunderstandings themselves become enshrined in language. An example was when the Anglo-Saxons came to Britain and began mixing with the indigenous Celts. They tried to communicate and quite naturally asked the names of the various rivers they came across. 'What is that?' they asked, pointing at a river. The Celts, however, thought that they were asking what their word for a river was, and said that it was 'afon' or 'avon'. Indeed, 'afon' is still the Welsh for 'river'. The Saxons, however, thought that they had learnt the local name for the river, and themselves called it the 'Avon'. That is why there are several different River Avons in the South of England. They are each really the 'River River'. This encapsulates the possibility of misunderstanding across languages and cultures. It also shows that an ability to communicate is parasitic on having a shared world. The Saxon could see and point to the same piece of water that the Celt was familiar with. They could each take for granted both that the river was there, and that the other could see it. The problem was whether the individual or generic name was being asked for. Such mutual misunderstanding could not be the norm without the possibility of translation being undermined. Conversely, accepting, as we surely must, that translation between different human languages is possible, we have to conclude that relativism is mistaken. We are not all locked in separate worlds, but live in one world and react to it in broadly similar ways.

The idea of different worlds is a consequence of a global relativism that, as we have seen, undermines the possibility of language. Even stating it involves using the resources of a language, which has to assume the falsity of relativism. One can never intelligibly claim the truth that there is no such thing as truth. Relativists may, however, persist by arguing that they are not after all involved in a contradiction. They would claim that they are saying it is merely true 'for him' or 'for her' that there is no such thing as absolute truth. The view that all truth is relative, it might be argued, is perfectly consistent, as long as objective truth is not claimed. How can that be inconsistent? The relativist might go on to point out an evident flaw in Plato's argument against Protagoras. Socrates is talking of Protagoras, and says that 'admitting as he does that everyone's opinion is true, he must acknowledge the truth of his opponents' belief about his own belief, when they think he is wrong'.[1] This, however, is an unfair argument. Protagoras held that everyone's opinion was true for the person holding it. His beliefs were true for him and it follows that his opponents' beliefs were not simply true, but true for them. The issue was not that because his opponents' views were true, his own had to be false. They could still be true for him, although they were not for them. There was no contradiction in people holding different views, even about the status of truth.

Yet despite this point, it is hard not to feel that there is a contradiction simmering beneath the surface. Protagoras does not have to admit he is wrong and his opponents right, but he surely has to accept it as a fact that he has opponents, who do not agree with him. It is hard to see why he is arguing with them if he does not. Yet once he accepts anything as a fact, particularly an unwelcome one, his relativism crumbles. The world is not, it seems, malleable in accordance with his beliefs. Whether people agree or not is part of an objective state of affairs. It is not just true for him that he has opponents. It is just true. The important point is not what his opponents believe or say, but the fact that they have the beliefs. Relativism, in its global form, cannot account even for such features of the world as other people's beliefs.

Perhaps, it might be said, global relativism is self-defeating. Asserting it is too much like sawing off the branch on which one is sitting. Might there not be other forms of relativism which are more convincing, just because they are less ambitious? The global relativism we have been considering has in fact embraced an ontological relativism, which makes reality dependent on belief and agreement. Convention and shared presuppositions determine the make-up of the world. This is tantamount to saying there is no world, only beliefs about it. Apart from the difficulty of saying what 'it' is, we seem to be left with a world consisting simply of different beliefs. That may be different from the ordinary world we thought we lived in, but it is still a world, where other people's beliefs and practices are not just a reflection of my own. They exist in their own right.

Another form of relativism can result from the reflection that languages seem to divide up the world differently. It can be pointed out, as Kuhn claimed, that scientific theories posit different entities. They are strictly incommensurable. That means that the terms of one theory cannot be reproduced in another. Classical physics cannot, for instance, describe sub-atomic events. Quantum mechanics, with its own conceptual apparatus, is completely different. Thus one could suggest that a conceptual relativism is in order, marking the distinctiveness of conceptual schemes. Yet this becomes a full-blooded relativism if it is assumed that we have no access to the world except through our concepts. In effect, our concepts then create our world. 'Nature' or 'the world' may then depend on how we happen to think about 'it'. As, by definition, conceptual schemes vary, we are once again being parcelled up into different compartments. There appears to be no access from one to the other, and nothing external to them, in virtue of which they can be compared.

This may all be too quick. 'Conceptual relativism' or 'conceptual relativity' may mean nothing more than that there are different patterns of thought, or different conceptual schemes. They offer different ways of understanding the world, but there need be no implication that our understanding somehow constructs the world. Science is a good example. It develops and changes, and new concepts, such as 'electron' or 'quark', have to be introduced. These cannot be translated into the terms of the earlier theories, as the whole point is that science progresses. Our knowledge increases and conceptual innovation is a part of that process. Scientists in the twenty-first century will not think in the same way as scientists did in the eighteenth century. That does not mean, though, that truth is relative. The physical world was the same three hundred years ago as it is now. Our ancestors just did not understand it as well. In the same way, different cultures may have different concepts, which make some translation more difficult. They all, though, have to deal with the same world and the same human nature. There are external constraints on the forming of the culture, and also an independent measure against which the understanding of different societies can be correlated.

It may be claimed that every such measurement begs the question. It will be our understanding against theirs. Why, it will be asked, can we be so sure we are right and they are wrong? Will we not, as the later Wittgenstein suggested, be merely using slogans against each other, or calling the others 'fools' or 'heretics'? Once the mere fact of cultural difference is admitted, why should we think that we are superior to others? The issue of conceptual differences is bound up with wider questions of what might be termed 'cultural relativism'.

The Incoherence of Relativism

Different societies have always had different customs. The old adage, 'When in Rome do as the Romans do', bears witness to this. Not everyone plays cricket or drives on the left-hand side of the road. Should we condemn those who differ from us merely because they are different? Some customs are harmless, but others are less so. Not many people were willing to accept that apartheid in South Africa was merely to be seen as a local custom to be understood in its own terms. Moral relativism, itself, is a fashionable species of relativism, which no doubt gives a spurious respectability to more global versions. Plato's disputes with Protagoras encompassed moral issues as well as wider issues about reality. Relativism can be applied at different levels, and it would be possible to be a relativist about morality and still accept that we all live in one world. Morality might be seen as on a par with other local customs and questions of etiquette. It is a matter of convention, of agreement, rather than of truth, even if the two can still be distinguished.

Customs change from place to place and over time. The wearing of hats on formal occasions is not now expected, whereas it used to be essential. Perhaps all morality is like that, it will be said. This is the edge of a vast debate, but it is dubious whether moral matters could ever be treated on a par with mere issues of 'polite' behaviour. The latter is very often totally constituted by convention. It is a matter merely of doing what everyone does. Morality, however, would seem to be much more concerned with what is good and bad, beneficial and harmful, for people. That is where agreement is not enough, but our customs come up against the brute, objective facts about the world we live in. People flourish or die no matter what our conventions. Moral relativism, itself, will gain much of its force from a wider relativism. It is surprisingly easy to be drawn from the limited relativism about morality to a more global view, according to which it is considered wrong to impose our view of the world on others. That quickly degenerates into the comfortable position that no one can claim a universal truth, but that all our beliefs are just 'true for' us.

Moral relativism, indeed, gains much of its impetus from a quest for tolerance. The idea that nothing can be thought right or wrong in itself, simply because it is considered wrong to impose one's views on others, is surprisingly popular. Yet this clearly involves an explicit and flagrant contradiction. The view that tolerance is good and intolerance bad means that there is at least one set of non-relative values. It is being said that we ought to be tolerant and that intolerant societies ought to be condemned. There are limits to the tolerance even of most liberals. That is because, if they genuinely believe in the importance of freedom, they cannot accept that those who attack freedom are right even 'for themselves'.

There are several stages in an argument about tolerating those who disagree with us. We may uphold the idea of truth and think our opponents are mistaken, but we may still think that they have a right to make their judgements. We would not impose our views on them by force. Indeed, genuine believers in truth must always be ready to consider that they may themselves be mistaken, wholly or partially. When we differ from others in any matter we may be able to learn from them, just as we might hope they could learn from us. We have seen how a realist, at any level, in morality or elsewhere, will always recognize that what we think and what is the case may be far apart. Yet for that very reason we always have to recognize that we ourselves may be wrong. We have good reason not to be arrogant. This is particularly important in science, where doctrines about the so-called 'social construction of science' suggest that scientific views merely reflect the social context of those holding them. They cannot then be about the world at all, or if they are, social influences can never be sifted out. We could thus never be sufficiently confident that we see physical reality as it is. As a result, it becomes more important who we are and where we are speaking from, than whether what we say is true. Yet the important point about science is not that it is a white, middle-class activity, even if it may be true that, in some societies, scientists happen to be in that category. Even the issue of whether there are enough female scientists is totally irrelevant to questions about the truth and reliability of any theory being advanced.

There can be little distance between what I believe and what I ought to accept, if truth is not at stake. For a relativist, who makes the norms of society the only standard, the only issues can be which society I belong to and whether my beliefs are correct by its standards. To revert to the metaphor of a game, I can break the rules, but they are the only measure. A Catholic who does not accept, say, the Virgin Birth, may be judged wrong by the standards of Catholic theology, and perhaps by wider Christian standards. Being a bad Catholic is one thing, however. The basic question should be whether Catholicism is propagating true beliefs. Is a virgin birth possible or, if possible, credible? There is plenty of room for argument here, but it is a different question from whether one is a loyal member of one's Church, merely going by the rules. Relativists can only allow a narrow space for error and mistake when I do not follow local norms properly. The only relevant issue remains whether I am living according to the relevant convention or rule.

Relativism encourages a seductive complacency. It is why science and relativism must be antagonistic to each other. Science must test and question. Its progress depends on criticism and free discussion. The mere enforcement of convention can be stultifying. It no doubt happens everywhere, and Kuhn's use of the term 'paradigm' suggests that even in science some conformity to prevailing wisdom may be a necessary stage in scientific progress. That, however, can only be a springboard for a future quest for new knowledge. We are in a dangerous position once, in science or elsewhere, we are satisfied with our views simply because that is the way we see things, rather than because we have some assurance of their truth. Conventions can be comfortable and reassuring. They can also be very misleading. Agreement may make for a quiet life, but it can encourage us to take more notice of what other people happen to think, rather than being willing to champion truth. Relativism can by definition have no room for prophets: they are breaking ranks and going against the established norms of belief and practice.

Even the view that relativism somehow encourages tolerance has to be questioned. Tolerance may often be advocated as the norm for everyone, but relativism has, by definition, to accept all existing societies and refrain from advocating new kinds. It has to tolerate difference. This so-called 'pluralism', celebrating differences, inevitably results in a refusal to distinguish between good and bad ones. Yet some societies, throughout history up to the present day, would seem far from admirable. The relativist cannot criticize Nazi Germany, or its imitators, or talk of human rights. 'Ethnic cleansing' may be a recognized practice in some places, but a relativist cannot seem to stand anywhere in order to condemn it. If it is a local norm, that is all, it seems, that can be said.

Relativists must always face one insuperable problem, irrespective of whether their relativism is specific, as in the case of morality, or wholly general. They can never recognize the fact of difference without abstracting themselves from the context in which they make that judgement. This presupposes that somehow they can be rationally detached from the various alternatives, whether they be kinds of morality, cultures or world-views. A relativist must implicitly claim to be able to be separated from them all, in order to see, and presumably to understand, their distinctive characters. A thorough-going relativist must be so embedded in one way of looking at things that it must surely be impossible to envisage radical alternatives. The idea that our culture or conceptual scheme completely governs the way we think must have the result that we cannot even see that anything else could be true.

Our society determines for us what the world is. That must be that, according to the relativist. The minute we see that our society's ways are not the only ones, and that other judgements about truth are possible, we are detaching ourselves from the thought-forms of a particular society. We are beginning to see our reasoning in ways that are not dictated by our social context. Alasdair MacIntyre, a leading contemporary philosopher, comments 'that generally only when traditions either fail and disintegrate or are challenged, do their adherents become aware of them as traditions, and begin to theorize about them'.[2] The very idea of one tradition amongst others suggests an opportunity for judgement and choice. It is hardly surprising that the Enlightenment stress on reason was coupled with the conscious repudiation of tradition. Once tradition is seen simply as a tradition, rather than as the only natural and right way to do things, its grip has already been loosened.

The paradox is that once relativists consciously hold to social norms merely on the grounds that they exist, they are, in effect, having to stand back from them, in order to recognize that they need not be bound by them. The very statement of relativism, however incoherent, itself demands the very kind of rational judgement about what is the case that relativism seems to undermine. We all have to see alternative possibilities and recognize the fact of different sets of beliefs and cultures. Relativism, as a diagnosis, would much more naturally fit the person who slavishly follows tradition without realizing it. Such people judge truth without understanding how their judgements are historically and socially conditioned. They would be so caught up with the assumptions of a particular time and place that no alternative would even seem possible. In other words, no one in that position would ever be able to assert relativism in the first place. Relativism cannot accept the idea of an impartial standpoint, a view that is not a view from somewhere, with all its limitations. Yet relativism, to be understood as a theory in the first place, needs just such a standpoint. It always demands a God's-eye point of view in order to survey the myriad sets of human beliefs. It then wishes to claim from such a position its portentous conclusion that there is no God's-eye point of view. In other words, relativism has to use a rationality, which is detached from context, to show us how reason must always be rooted in its context.

Notes

1 *Theaetetus*, 171a
2 Alasdair MacIntyre, *Whose Justice, Which Rationality?* Duckworth, London, 1998, p. 8.

6

The Impact of Darwinism

Relativism and Scientism

Postmodernism and forms of relativism concentrate on human beliefs and culture, on what can be taught and transmitted in a society. This makes it easy to conclude that societies can vary radically from each other, and that they are free to set their own standards. There has always been a tug in the study of human society between those who want to explain it in its own terms, and those who wish to base it on some general scientific understanding, which embeds human society in the natural world. This is a philosophical dispute about the basis and purpose of social science: is it in the business of the interpretation and understanding of cultural differences, or should it rather be itself rooted in the natural sciences?

The dispute between a relativism where anything goes, and a quest for scientific explanation, can become polarized. The choice may seem to be that either one thinks the truth is in the eye of the beholder, so that one can believe anything without fear of mistake, or on the other hand, one has to turn to the alleged certainties of science. Once modern science is seen as the true heir of Enlightenment thinking, that choice can seem to be between arbitrary belief and reason, between relativism and science.

This opposition can be stressed too much because, as we have already seen, there are plenty who would relegate science itself to being a Western form of thought. It can be made to look a product of a particular type of society at a particular time. If reason can be classified as a category of the Enlightenment, then so can science. Yet many who admit that they themselves follow the precepts of the Enlightenment would see science as a bul-

wark against relativism. E. O. Wilson, for example, draws a contrast between postmodernism and the Enlightenment by saying: 'Enlightenment
thinkers believe we can know everything, and radical postmodernists believe we can know nothing'.[1] The retreat from truth, hence knowledge, is
clear enough in postmodernism. Optimism and trust in human reason were
certainly features of the eighteenth-century Enlightenment. Once God was
removed from the picture, humans became the arbiters of reality. The anthropocentric nature of thought became all too apparent, so that everything
beyond human grasp was liable to be dismissed as irrelevant.

The idea that human reason itself sets the standards, without any external
constraint or guidance, is an unstable one. There may not be any problems as
long as reason retains its self-confidence, and does not question the basis of
its own legitimacy. Once, though, the status of human rationality is questioned, the question must arise as to what might give it any legitimacy. What
warrants our trust in it? This question has a greater force when we look at
the status of contemporary science as the expression of human reason.
Postmodernism denies the whole conception of human rationality and its
ability to provide any overarching framework, or 'metanarrative', according
to which we should all live our lives. Yet if there are no universal truths to
be discovered, where does this leave science? It may not be surprising that
those who recoil from the abyss opened up in front of them by postmodernism
are willing to turn back to the universal claims of science. The latter seem to
offer the most plausible antidote to nihilism. A new impetus has thus been
provided to a materialism, or naturalism, which has long given science pride
of place.

The choice between the irrationalism of postmodernity and the vaunted
rationalism of science is probably too stark. They are two extremes, and
rejecting one does not mean that one has to accept the other. They have one
thing in common. The reduction of truth to beliefs, and the placing of reason in particular social contexts, means that we can describe beliefs in a kind
of cultural commentary. Philosophy, however, as the exercise of reason,
must then be an illusion. It can only appear as part of the general procession
of beliefs and thoughts. In other words, we can only aspire to give a history
of ideas. In so far as we are ourselves embedded in a context, even the
prospect of giving that kind of detached and intellectual history seems remote. Once we turn to science, on the other hand, we see that science itself
demands a monopoly of reason. Its empirical method is seen as the very
essence of rationality. The result is that just as metaphysics, and philosophical
reasoning in general, have to be dismissed by postmodernism, we find that

'scientism', the trust that science alone is the source of knowledge, also allows no room for philosophy. Of its nature, the latter involves a form of reasoning that does not depend on particular facts. It logically precedes science. Naturalist attempts to make it an 'under-labourer' for science put a large question mark by the whole future of philosophy as a separate discipline.

At its most ambitious, indeed, science does not just trust in its own resources. It can aspire to explain human rationality itself. Since science is an expression of that rationality, this means that it has itself to explain the conditions which makes science itself possible. Whether this circularity, according to which scientific method explains the very existence of scientific modes of reasoning, is self-defeating, is a major shadow over the whole enterprise. Attempts to explain away human reason, rather than to accept it at face value, run into the same kind of difficulty as an assault on the possibility of reasoning produced by relativism. Anything which appears to disconnect reason and truth, by relating reason to social context or by giving it a scientific explanation, raises the issue of how far there are good reasons for such an apparent belittling of reason.

Darwinism

Why should a scientific explanation of human reasoning disconnect it from truth? What would such a scientific explanation look like anyway? It is here that the importance is clear of Charles Darwin, the mid-nineteenth century proponent of evolution through natural selection. Although he was not a philosopher but a biologist, his ideas have become ever more influential in ways that go to the heart of philosophy as the years have gone on. It was in his famous *Origin of Species*, published in 1859, that he sketched in a few sentences the possible relevance of this belief in evolution to wider issues. He said: 'In the distant future, I see open fields for more important researches. Psychology will be based on a new foundation, that of the necessary requirement of each mental power and capacity by gradation. Light will be thrown on the origin of man and his history.'[2]

In Darwin's time the mechanisms by which natural selection might operate were far from clear. The transmission of genes was not understood, and indeed it was not until the discovery of DNA that the full role of genes as the building blocks of life could begin to be seen. Genes are the smallest replicable parts of DNA. They are passed on through the generations, and the process of natural selection will determine which of them are spread through the gene pool and which are winnowed out. With the mapping of the human genome, the part genetic inheritance plays in the moulding of humans is becoming better understood. The links between genes and disease are crucial, but genes always operate in a context. They react to an environment. They may predispose individuals to certain illnesses, but environmental factors often provide the necessary trigger. Not everyone reacts to the same environmental factors in the same way. Genetic influences may enable one person to withstand a threat that proves fatal to someone else. We know that radioactivity can be instrumental in causing various forms of cancer. Yet at Hiroshima some who were nearer the atomic blast did not contract leukaemia, while others further away did. The interaction of genes and environment is subtle and multi-faceted.

Neo-Darwinism sees the operation of natural selection on different sets of genes as a basic form of explanation. Some genes make people fitter in their environment than others do. The former enable people to survive and reproduce, and their genes will spread. There is an in-built mechanism of selection, but it is not a matter of purpose or intention. One gene will prove beneficial in a particular environment and spread. Another will happen to be harmful and those organisms which possess it will fail to compete successfully. When a particular species of animal, such as deer, needs to be a fast runner to escape predators, genes giving it strength and speed will tend to spread amongst the species. Slow and weak deer will not live long enough to reproduce. Deer attracted to mates with strength and speed, and the physical characteristics giving rise to them, will then be able to spread their own genes, including those encouraging that attraction. Such qualities will inevitably be selected and their opposites will tend to disappear.

This is all a consequence of natural selection. It may look as if there is a driving purpose behind it, but that is just how things work out. A result is that in the matching of genes to environment, much depends on the environment. Catastrophic and sudden change will leave organisms which are suited for one set of circumstances struggling in another. Evolution itself depends on a certain regularity and order. There can be major disasters, such as meteors crashing into the earth. Species can be, and have been, wiped out. Extraordinary climatic change can obviously be a problem. The development of species is, therefore, a historical, rather than a law-governed, process, and it depends on particular circumstances. Life could not have developed without a certain stability and species could not have gained a footing in their various ecological niches. A gene, selected for in a particular environment, will only be beneficial to the organism which inherits it if the environment, with all its challenges and opportunities, has remained roughly the same. Shaggy coats will be unhelpful in a hotter climate. White fur will be less useful if the snow melts.

Daniel Dennett, an American philosopher, says:

> If I were to give an award for the single best idea anyone has ever had, I'd give it to Darwin, ahead of Newton and Einstein and everyone else. In a single stroke, the idea of evolution by natural selection unifies the realm of life, meaning, and purpose, with the realm of space and time, cause and effect, mechanism and physical law.[3]

It is perhaps indicative of Dennett's approach that, even though a philosopher, he automatically looks only to scientists as the source of great ideas. Yet the point he makes is important. Many people see in what is termed neo-Darwinism not only a scientific theory about gene selection, but a view which explains the whole of life. It does so in terms of mindless mechanisms working through biochemistry in a web of cause and effect. Although evolution was often thought in Victorian times to go hand in hand with progress, in fact there can be no direction given in any natural selection. Such patterns as there are can only be seen with the benefit of hindsight, and reflect the conditions of the past. One example, often referred to, is the way in which the wings of moths became darker in colour during the Industrial Revolution in the north of England so that they would still be camouflaged against tree trunks made black by pollution. Yet once measures were taken in the middle of the twentieth century to make the air cleaner, gradually the trunks of trees have returned to their normal colour, and the wings of moths have also had to become lighter through the generations, if they are to retain their camouflage.

Richard Dawkins, the evolutionary biologist, used the title *The Blind Watchmaker* for one of his books. He meant to draw attention to the way in which chance, rather than purpose, governs biological mechanisms. We have already remarked how the idea of a watch suggests something which has been purposely designed and manufactured. Similarly, the notion of any watchmaker, blind or not, suggests a role for intention and direction. Neo-Darwinism can allow no such notion, as Dawkins fully recognizes. Even the evolution of complexity is a problem for a Darwinian viewpoint. It is tempting to imagine some in-built natural bias for the evolution of more complex organisms. Yet simple organisms, like amoebae, continue to exist and flourish. Why should there be any tendency to produce more and more complex forms of life, ending with humans, endowed with brains that are somehow able to question and even try to make sense of it all?

Modern biology has set its face against any idea of ends in view, or of direction or purpose. It looks for causes and mechanisms, not reasons or functions. It is not teleological in the way that Aristotle's biology was. Natural selection, according to biology, is not a subtle device for producing us. Humans happened to appear as a result of a particular combination of events. If we 're-ran' biological history, like a film, it could all have unfolded again very differently. Each step in the process is part of a long chain of causes and effects in which chance is thought to play a leading role. Above all, genetic mutations give the opportunity for selection to explore new possibilities. Even this way of putting it makes the mindless and mechanical process which many biologists talk about look too deliberate and directed. Dennett talks of 'a set of individually mindless steps succeeding each other without the help of any intelligent supervision'.[4] Each genetic modification, however slight, will have consequences for an organism which will be tested in its environment. Gradually, so the story goes, more and more complex organisms will be produced.

Dennett uses the image of a crane, which contrasts with what he terms 'skyhooks', defined as 'miraculous lifters, unsupported and insupportable'.[5] As Dennett remarks, the idea may have connections with that of a *deus ex machina*, the god swung in on a crane at the end of some Greek tragedies to sort out a tangled situation: the tragedian presumably found that he could not solve the problems himself within the resources of the story. Real cranes rest on the ground and are firmly rooted in reality. Through their agency, even vast skyscrapers can be gradually raised up. For Dennett, Darwinism provides the mechanism, the crane, by which, through genetic modification interacting with the environment, life, including humans, evolved. His naturalism precludes any intervention from outside, particularly by God. It dismisses any idea that information is provided for the biological system from any external sources. Even the most complicated forms of life evolved from the simplest by a process not unlike pulling oneself up by one's own bootstraps. All causes are material, and all change is to be completely understood in terms of them.

A consequence of this position is that nothing is regarded as sacrosanct, even the development of the human mind and consciousness. Whereas relativism is content to investigate the fact of different beliefs, without speculating about any underlying physical explanation, naturalism in general, and neo-Darwinism in particular, have great ambitions. It is possible to give an evolutionary explanation for the development of intelligence, particularly when it is coupled with the growth in the size of the human brain during evolution. A certain understanding of one's situation can be coupled with the ability to adapt oneself to changing circumstances and to formulate different courses of action as one's surroundings dictate. This will help to improve the chances of one's own survival and the ability to look after one's family. Human reasoning, at least at its most basic level, can counteract other disadvantages, such as lack of speed when escaping from danger. More intelligent human beings would outwit the less intelligent, and a path could be set for an exponential growth in brain size through natural selection. As Nicholas Rescher, an American philosopher, says: 'We are so smart, because this is necessary for us to be here at all'.[6]

A Vicious Circle

Neo-Darwinism is not just concerned with how we obtained the capacities we possess. It is far more ambitious and wants to give a global explanation for how human minds work and for why we have the beliefs we naturally do. Above all, under the guise of so-called evolutionary epistemology, it wishes to explain why our minds and the world seem to fit together so well, and why our beliefs can be generally reliable. This would itself be a significant philosophical success. An old threat has been that of scepticism. How do any of us know that what we think bears any relation to the truth?

Relativism itself is a classical sceptical position claiming that there is no principled way of settling disagreement. Philosophy is always looking for some argument to show why human belief matches up with the world. Theists might say, with Descartes, that God, who has made us, would not deceive us. We have been endowed, it is argued, with the right apparatus to be able to arrive at true beliefs about the world, and even perhaps about God. Reason is then a divine gift. Once, however, this avenue has been blocked by naturalists, they have to come up with an alternative explanation. We do not just believe what we believe. That, in fact, is not far from the position of American pragmatists. They are fond of the slogan 'start from where you are'. We always, they say, have to take some beliefs for granted and cannot question everything at once. We need somewhere firm to stand, even if the only justification for standing there rather than somewhere else is that that is where we happen to be. A famous analogy put forward by pragmatists is of rebuilding a wooden boat when one is already at sea in it. One has, it is said, to stand on one set of planks while replacing another set. The point is, though, that we can change position. No planks, and no set of beliefs, are irreplaceable, as long as one does not try to replace them all simultaneously.

A Danish boat builder with philosophical inclinations once assured me that it would be impossible, in fact, to rebuild a boat in this fashion. He claimed that, as one might expect, one always needs to stand on dry ground in a shipyard. In the same way, if we merely accept all our beliefs at face value, and have nowhere firm to stand, we avoid the difficult question of whether they are actually about anything. We need, it seems, somewhere else to stand in order to survey our beliefs as a whole. As humans, we seem to need an independent assurance that our beliefs do match up with the real world. At this point, philosophers divide between those who want an assurance like this, whether they think it possible or not, and those who give up the quest. Naturalists, and in particular those who have taken up neo-Darwinian thinking, hold that such a metaphysical grounding must be an illusion. We can, they think, never get outside the ordinary beliefs we, as a species, have evolved to possess. Further, they would point to evolution, not just as the mechanism by which we have acquired the beliefs, but as a source of assurance that the beliefs are accurate.

How does this work? First, there is the general argument that, as an evolved species, we should expect that our brains, and their products, would fit the world. Our brains are adaptive mechanisms, helping us to survive; otherwise, it is claimed, they would not have developed as they did. Unless there is a general fit between brain and world, it is difficult to see how this would have occurred. There is, of course, an ongoing assumption that beliefs and other mental states can be reduced in some way to talk of brain processes. There is the further question why human consciousness was advantageous at all during evolution. Could not unconscious belief and reflex action have protected an organism just as well? We shall return to this point, but for the moment the issue appears to be simply the general connection between the brain, including all mental events, and the world.

Why is the world such that it can be understood by us? Second, how is it that we are able to obtain an understanding of it? Evolutionary mechanisms may have 'programmed' us with certain beliefs. The analogy with a computer programme, however, should not trap us into thinking that anyone or anything is deliberately in charge of the programming. One general argument, when confronted with the first question, is that evolution by natural selection would be impossible in a world which did not have regular and orderly processes. We could not have evolved to deal with a state of affairs that did not exist. There must be an inherent stability, and hence intelligibility, to provide the conditions necessary for evolution to occur.

It is often pointed out that at the social level there is indeed a gap between the state of society and the attitudes which evolved long ago to deal with situations long past. Basic desires and fears evolved over many thousands of years to equip us for a society of hunter-gatherers. A child might therefore very likely have an innate fear of snakes, but be inquisitive about an electric socket, which could be every bit as dangerous. The emotional equipment needed for an ancient mode of life may not be adequate in the confines of a modern metropolis. The physical world, however, has not changed, it will be argued, and its physical laws, together with the general reliability of nature, still hold good. The general physical conditions which underlay natural selection from earliest times still obtain, otherwise humans could not even now survive. Whatever changes there have been could only have occurred within strict limits. The mere fact that we are all able to survive and flourish is a guarantee, it seems, that our beliefs, even if hard-wired, are still reliable.

This is an argument about the reliability of our basic understanding about the world we live in. How do we know that the world, as we perceive it, bears any relation to the real world? The simple answer, according to evolutionary epistemology, is that the conditions which helped form human knowledge still hold, otherwise we could not continue to live. If people, like animals, do not see predators, they are liable to get eaten by them. I must be able to recognize a lion if there is one in front of me. Similarly, if a great chasm opened up in front of me, I will fall into it unless I see it. Systematically misleading perceptions will literally lead to our downfall. Just as evolution could not occur in the first place without a background of a certain level of stability and order, we could not survive as individuals unless we can see things as they are. The physical world is presumably not a dream and it must therefore be recognizable by us. We must be aware of its characteristics in order to survive.

All the arguments for stability and order as a background to evolution have themselves to assume the truth of the theory of evolution. Given that we have all evolved, we can deduce a lot about the conditions necessary for evolution through natural selection. Naturalists accept the truth of the neo-Darwinian picture because they see it as upheld by contemporary science. They draw philosophical conclusions about the nature of the world, indeed the whole universe, as a result of a particular scientific theory. They think that only empirical knowledge obtained through scientific method can be reliable. Philosophy or pure reason cannot, they believe, itself be a source of such knowledge. Why, though, should the truth of the theory of evolution be assumed in the first place? This is not a question about the arguments for or against evolution within science. It is a philosophical question about what enables them to assume that the theory does manage to encapsulate the on-going processes of the real world. The theory is itself the product of the human mind. Before we can adopt it, we have to take up a position about the human ability to come into contact with the real world. What is the relationship between mind and world? The answer cannot be given through the medium of the theory of evolution by natural selection. To hold the theory in the first place we will have to assume an ability on our part to understand the nature of reality. We have to trust human reason. Yet that is what the theory, through evolutionary epistemology, has been used to show. We seem to be involved in a massive circle. We are in touch with the world because we have evolved to be. How do we know we have evolved? The theory of evolution tells us so. How would we know the theory offers a true account of the world? The answer is that it is because our minds are attuned to the world and that is the result of evolution. So we go on.

Causes and Content

Part of the problem is the urge of the naturalist to give weight to a particular scientific theory, without being willing to stand back and ask what legiti-mizes science in the first place. Some philosophers would claim that no such question is necessary. Science is on top and that is all that can be said. Nicholas Rescher called the mechanism of scientific reasoning 'the most developed and sophisticated of our probative methods'. He continues: 'No elaborate argumentation is necessary to establish the all too evident fact that science has come out on top in the competition of rational selection with respect to alternative processes for substantiating and explaining our factual claims.'[7] It is intriguing that he uses the image of selection amongst competing alterna-tives. It is an illustration of how the categories of evolutionary theory domi-nate even descriptions of how science can be justified.

Rescher's approach is the pragmatist one of saying we are where we are, and that any deeper philosophical questioning is unnecessary. This is always unsatisfactory, since we can usually take up some other position, such as an opposition to science. The problem is why we should not do so. Relying on images of 'rational selection', in fact, only makes an appeal to evolutionary theory by using it as an analogy. The question is whether a scientific theory can actually explain how we do think and even how we should think. The point is not the simple one that rational argument may often involve intellectual competition like that between organisms. The fittest idea, like the fittest organism, would then survive. The more ambitious programme wants to use science to explain the content of our reasoning in terms of the way it has actually evolved.

A programme like that, it will be alleged, will always beg one of the most basic questions of all, namely the relation of mind to physical world. It may help to assume that the mind is just a part of the physical world, and that the physical processes of the brain, even at the sub-atomic level, are attuned to physical events simply because they are the same kind of thing. Talking in this way of neuronal events in the brain is one thing, however, but it is light years away from talk of understanding and reasoning, let alone the holding of scientific theories. The latter are conceptual, and seem to be different in kind from the web of physical cause and effect.

The content of belief is made irrelevant by evolutionary explanation. Genes are physical and have to have physical effects to have an influence on survival and reproduction. This mode of explanation will always stress genetic causes of behaviour. Beliefs would only be relevant in so far as they lead us to do one thing rather than another. They will be selected for if they have beneficial effects. They will eventually be winnowed out in the competition between organisms of varying fitness if they are harmful. Neo-Darwinian explanations tend to follow the same pattern, whether they are explaining the behaviour of bees in a hive, or the importance of religion in human society. Indeed if the content of beliefs and issues about truth were given prominence, sociobiology (or evolutionary psychology, as it is now usually called) would be forced to admit its own limitations. Its explanations would be far less comprehensive in scope.

Neo-Darwinian explanations may produce patterns of explanation which we can use to talk of the struggle of ideas. Some thinkers have tried to define units of culture as 'memes', involved in a struggle for selection by analogy with genes. Whether culture can be divided up in this artificial way is another matter. What a neo-Darwinian explanation certainly cannot do is distinguish between different ideas and beliefs when they have similar effects. For instance, religion always provides a difficulty for naturalists who want to give an evolutionary account of society, in the strong sense of relating social behaviour with genes. By definition, traditional religion is totally opposed to views ruling out anything non-physical. To a materialist it is therefore self-evidently false. Yet religion persists in human society and can claim to be a virtually universal phenomenon across cultures. Why should it exist at all? Evolutionary explanations would have to be able to show why it should have continued and not been selected against long ago. The only apparent alternative, which is unpalatable to the ambitious neo-Darwinian, is to accept that such facets of human society lie far beyond the scope of biological explanation.

Religion appears to encourage altruistic behaviour, sometimes of an extreme kind, involving self-sacrifice. Yet laying down my life for others cannot be seen as a piece of behaviour that could be under genetic control. Unless I save the lives of close relatives who are liable to have shared the genes prompting such behaviour, my genes would not spread through such action. Neither they nor I could gain advantage from it, as I would cease to exist. Genes encouraging any kind of self-destructive behaviour, or even unselfish behaviour benefiting others, could not easily be transmitted through the generations. Genes encouraging youthful suicide or total celibacy are unlikely to exist, since they would not easily be transmitted through the generations. Those who possess them would not be able to help them on their way. This makes it even more mysterious why sets of false belief, which may appear to encourage behaviour that is harmful from an evolutionary point of view, can exist and even flourish. The materialist has to face this question, and the only answer could be that religious belief has survival value, even if its content is unacceptable. Whether or not this is plausible, there are two particular morals for our purposes. The first is that no neo-Darwinian explanation could distinguish between different theological claims. All that matters is the fact that a belief is held and the effects it has. When different beliefs and even different religions have the same results, they have to be treated as identical. The second moral, arising out of this, is that truth has completely dropped out of account. It does not matter if a belief is true or false, as long as it is useful, from a genetic point of view. That does not stop the materialist wanting to assume that religion is false.

These are just some examples of a tremendous problem for evolutionary epistemology. This may masquerade as an epistemology, talking of the warrant for holding certain beliefs, but it is much more inclined to talk of causes rather than reasons. It is more interested in what has made us believe something than in whether we ought to continue believing it. It is concerned with the evolutionary effects of belief. The contents of consciousness become irrelevant except in so far as they affect behaviour. They then play no independent role in the theory, which will look at the conditions for the transmission of genes and for the production of relevant behaviour. By definition, if genes, as part of the physical world, control our behaviour in such a way that they are replicated and spread through the gene pool, the contents of all our beliefs are irrelevant. The line of explanation runs from genes to behaviour. Anything intervening does not just complicate the explanation, but undermines it. It brings in an independent variable not required by the form of explanation. If, in other words, I act because of my beliefs and not because of my genes, genetic explanation is squeezed out. Either a belief in God is important or it is not. A belief like that could have no proper function of its own if it is simply caused by my genes and in turn causes my behaviour. It does not itself have the power to alter anything. From the point of view of neo-Darwinian theory it is redundant, a wheel that is not really needed to turn anything. The theory cannot afford to be concerned with the nature of belief at all. It need only be concerned with its effect and not its content.

A belief in neo-Darwinism is liable to erode any trust in the efficacy of belief. The point is not just about belief alone, but about the relevance of reason. Rational creatures have gained an important evolutionary advantage over those that are unable to reason but act through blind instinct. Once, however, ideas of natural selection are applied to particular judgements, the focus is on their effects and not their content. Yet where does this leave the reasoning which brings thinkers to a belief in evolution? They may think that they can close the philosophical gap between mind and world. We have to have true beliefs to enable us to survive. The example of religion, in some neo-Darwinian theory, however, shows that as long as beliefs are advantageous, they do not have to be true. There need be no direct connection between reason and truth.

Our trust in the reliability of reason must be undermined once we accept this. Reproductive success may help to reinforce the holding of certain beliefs and truth becomes irrelevant. Why then should we put any of our trust in neo-Darwinian theory in the first place? If it is correct, those putting it forward, whether they are aware of this or not, must be more concerned with their own genetic interest than with truth. Perhaps money that they acquire from their books and television appearances will enable them to obtain glamorous wives (or handsome husbands) and bring up large families. This may seem an unfair attack on their integrity, but that may indicate that the pursuit of truth has to be a more selfless and detached activity than their own theory can allow. According to them, rationality is a means to other ends. We are thus faced with a problem. Either a global Darwinism is true, or it is not. If it is, the reasons given in its support may be unreliable and we may find we are being manipulated. If it is not, then we should take no notice of it. The theory, if true, may not be one that can be consistently argued for in a rational manner.

What is going wrong here is that a scientific theory has been given a global, and philosophical, function. We started with harmful genetic effects brought about by a certain kind of behaviour, such as incest. A general connection between genes and behaviour has then been forged into a much closer link. It has ballooned into a theory about how the mind works, with genes dictating how we think. We began with an empirical theory that makes interesting points about how we cannot behave for long in ways that stop the transmission of genes through the generations. Naturalism has exploited this until it becomes an explanation of the very functioning of rationality.

In Dennett's words, Darwin's 'dangerous idea' about evolution acts as a 'universal acid', eating through everything, even our most cherished beliefs about ourselves. He asks:

> If mindless evolution could account for the breathtakingly clever artefacts of the biosphere, how could our own 'real' minds be exempt from an evolutionary explanation? Darwin's idea thus threatened to spread all the way up, dissolving the illusion of our own authorship, our own divine spark of creativity and understanding.[8]

Dennett is happy to help the process along. Yet he is putting forward something far wider than a particular scientific theory. Its global relevance, reaching far beyond the possibility of ordinary scientific testing and measurement, is such that it is clearly a philosophical, not a scientific, position. Any attempt to rely on scientific evidence and theories alone would result in a much more cautious approach. Dennett, and others, use philosophical reasoning to show the irrelevance of such reasoning. Yet if reason is redundant or ineffectual, so are the rational arguments that claim to show that it is. Our individual creativity may be given a scientific explanation, along with our ability to distinguish truth from falsity, or the real from the unreal. It may then seem as if philosophy has given way to science. Yet all the old problems then return with even greater urgency. What grounds have we for thinking that human science is reliable? Why should scientists be in a better position than anyone else to have contact with the real world? How is science possible in the first place, without a reliance on human reason? We shall have to explore further the presuppositions which incline so many to be disdainful of a philosophical answer to these questions.

Notes

1 E. O. Wilson, *Consilience*, Alfred A. Knopf, New York, 1998, p. 40.
2 Charles Darwin, *On the Origin of Species*, Penguin Books, Harmondsworth, p. 458.
3 Daniel Dennett, *Darwin's Dangerous Idea*, Simon and Schuster, New York, 1995, p. 21.
4 Ibid., p. 59.
5 Ibid., p. 75.
6 Nicholas Rescher, *A System of Pragmatic Idealism, Vol. 1, Human Knowledge in Idealistic Perspective*, Princeton University Press, Princeton, NJ, 1992, p. 41.
7 Ibid., p. 178.
8 Dennett, *Darwin's Dangerous Idea*, p. 63.

7

The Challenge of Determinism

The Limits of Causation?

Naturalism, as a philosophical position, holds that the physical world is self-contained and not open to any external, or 'supernatural', influences. The causal closure of the physical domain is, in fact, a basic requirement for materialists. If a physical event has a cause, that cause must be a physical one. We can only find explanations of events in the physical world within the physical world and in physical terms. This way of putting things leaves open whether all physical events do have causes. Certainly quantum mechanics suggests that they do not. There may be statistical irregularities among, say, microscopic entities, so that they maintain stability at the level of the world we are familiar with. That does not mean that each movement of each particle is predictable or determined. It may well be random and uncaused.

The image of cranes, rather than 'skyhooks', drawing on the processes of evolution may be a powerful one in the defence of physical rather than supernatural causation. It suggests that science should not expect to come across miraculous interventions from outside the physical system. Yet the image essentially contrasts different kinds of causes. Skyhooks are rather like cranes, except that they are miraculous ones. They do not have any support and they certainly do not rest on the earth. We have to face up to two questions, namely whether there could be non-physical causes (or 'skyhooks') and whether all explanation is causal anyway. Any naturalism worthy of the name will not just dismiss skyhooks, but will be inclined to assimilate all forms of explanation to physical explanation. It is hardly surprising that the only alternative to ordinary causation which a naturalist or materialist could conceive is some sort of ghostly copy. They assume that if there is not a physical crane, there must be some sort of mechanism just like it, only outside the normal processes of the material world.

This belief in causation as the only proper model of explanation runs very deep. It functions on the same level as explaining the movement of billiard balls after one has struck the other. Indeed, the idea of atoms as little balls bumping into and pushing each other has always been seductive. It is still very difficult to realize that sub-atomic particles may be real and yet not behave like that at all. They may even be able to influence each other from a distance. Yet the concept of reality has been so entwined with those of ordinary cause and effect through contact that this has been much contested. It has been hard to accept something as real that behaves very differently from the objects in our familiar world.

In the seventeenth century a belief in the 'corpuscular' nature of matter led very easily to the idea that perhaps relations between these ultimate particles of matter could explain everything. John Locke faced up to the question of 'thinking matter' and considered the claim that even God could be a material being. The issue was whether the mere rearrangement of bits of stuff could somehow explain thought. Indeed, could that itself be thought? Analogous problems can arise today in connection with whether computers can think. Locke's view was that to imagine that an eternal, thinking Being who could be composed of particles of matter, each of which could not think, would be absurd. Thought could then, he maintained, only arise because of the way they were arranged. Yet moving small bits of matter around in different combinations may seem very far from active, purposive reasoning. How could mere differences of position amongst different 'corpuscles' result in coherent thought, let alone knowledge? Moreover, if the motion of the various parts somehow produced thinking, Locke suggested that all thoughts must be 'unavoidably accidental'. Each part would not be able to think, and in fact the thought of the whole could only be the chance result of the movement of the parts. Thinking is then defined in terms that seem totally irrelevant to the content of any thought. Locke continued:

Freedom, power, choice and all rational and wise thinking or acting will be quite taken away. So that such a thinking Being will be no better nor wiser, than pure blind matter: since to render all into the accidental, unguided motions of blind matter, or into thought depending on unguided motions of blind matter, is the same thing.[1]

Locke could not see how rational thought and choice can arise out of the realm of physical cause and effect. Matter is blind, in that it cannot understand what it is doing or why it is doing it. It merely reacts to other stimuli and produces effects. It follows that its 'motions' are not deliberate, but accidental. A materialist would retort that Locke is dealing with a primitive physical theory. Our experience with computers and our increasing knowledge of the working of the brain should surely be relevant. We can now see, it might be suggested, the intimate connection, and perhaps even the identity, between arrangements of matter and our own reasoning and thought. Yet, however sophisticated modern theories may become, the principle and the problem remain the same. Are we not changing the subject when we pass from talking about physical activity, whether in the brain or elsewhere, to talking about trains of thought? Locke was envisaging a situation in which the content of thought could be explained only in terms of the motion of physical particles. They governed the thought, so that what we are thinking becomes an irrelevant by-product. The language of the present day might be different, referring, say, to neurons, but the idea is the same. What we think and how we reason is the result of our brain processes and not the cause. They may, indeed, simply *be* those processes, but in any case, they are certainly not independent of them. There is no spiritual entity guiding our brain and no 'self' in control. Whatever the status of the contents of our minds, they are subject to what goes on in our brains, and our brains behave according to the laws of physics. They are no different from any other part of the physical world.

This is a significant step because it suggests that physical laws govern how we think, together with everything else that goes on in our minds. They thus can explain everything. It has been an article of faith for empiricist philosophers from the time of Hume in the eighteenth century that causal explanation is the only proper kind of explanation. The alternative is to imagine events to be random or accidental. Our actions are seen as totally inexplicable unless we are caused to act. Otherwise what we do will be seen as random as the unpredictable behaviour of a sub-atomic particle. Yet, as Hume stressed, our whole life depends on the knowledge that human nature remains constant and that we can understand how people are likely to behave. He points out that anyone who at noon leaves his purse full of gold on the pavement at Charing Cross, in the middle of London, is not likely to find it there if he goes back an hour later. Hume's own words are that 'he may as well expect that it will fly away like a feather as that he will find it untouched'.[2] Things have not changed in the intervening centuries and people can still be just as greedy and dishonest. The issue is whether just because there are tendencies and regularities in how we behave, we are totally predictable, and indeed not free to do otherwise than we do. The suggestion that an uncaused action must be random and pointless helps the argument. It seems that we either understand other people's actions in terms of causes, or we do not understand them at all. Actions have to be explained in terms of physical causes, or else in terms of some shadowy copy of a physical cause, still pulling and pushing in a physical way. The snag is that, as the latter is by definition not physical, this can be quickly dismissed as incoherent. The temptation remains, though, to think of rational behaviour only on a causal model.

Thinking that the accidental and the random are the same as not being caused is very strange. Accidents can certainly be caused, as anyone involved in a traffic accident is only too well aware. They may not be intended, but that is a different, though important, matter. Computers can equally be programmed to make random choices. Even if the choice may be caused, the content is not determined. The computer might have to pick any number between one and fifty, without being told which number. There might be a physical explanation for the choosing of a number, as the computer is a physical machine. We have to distinguish between this and the fact that the number itself may be unpredictable. What we can predict and what is caused are not the same. Prediction lies in the realm of what we, as humans, can know or find out. Causation, on the other hand, may far outstrip our own human abilities to track it. It may still be a fact.

This last point is the philosophical one about determinism. As I have already argued in chapter 4, determinism is a global, even metaphysical, position, and is not amenable to empirical proof or physical checking. We can never know from experience that because we have not so far uncovered a cause that means that there is not one, or that we should give up looking. The issue of the limits of causation is a typically philosophical one. It has become particularly relevant with the question of indeterminacy in quantum mechanics. Even in that case, some physicists have been reluctant to give up their belief in determinism. Similarly, argument still rages in chaos theory over the precise philosophical relevance of the fact that there are limits to the possibility of prediction, when we cannot have precise knowledge of the intricate initial conditions of an event. This is important for weather forecasting, among other areas, where, as we have seen, infinitesimally small local variations can eventually be amplified into catastrophic effects, such as hurricanes.

Blind Matter

Do gaps in our knowledge have to mean gaps in the causal framework of the world? There may be real gaps in physical processes, when the procession of cause and effect breaks down. The problem is that we cannot distinguish between such a case and one where we are merely ignorant of actual causes. Physicists could go on positing 'hidden variables' in quantum mechanics in the absence of any experimental evidence. They could go on positing unknown causes for the apparently random behaviour of particles. The issue becomes in the end a philosophical one, concerning our conception of the nature of the world. That does not mean it is trivial, or can be dismissed by scientists. Such philosophical positions both implicitly and explicitly govern the whole approach of science. Disputes about the extent of causation have to be settled by philosophical means.

Some think that determinism is an empirical thesis and they question its philosophical standing. They think that even if it has not yet been shown to be true, it could be, because one day gaps in our knowledge will be filled. Our knowledge could be extended, at least in principle, they would hold, and we should certainly not place artificial, or philosophical, obstacles in the way. Yet what does it mean to think that something could happen in principle, even if it could never happen in fact? We are only too aware of intrinsic limits on the possibility of human knowledge in certain areas. When minute differences can have great effects, we can always suppose that knowledge of a measurement to another decimal place would be important for our ability to predict. Measurement can always be more accurate, since precision is a matter of degree. Weather forecasting will always face the problem that it is impossible to give an absolutely exhaustive and precise account of what is happening everywhere in the country at a time of unsettled weather, let alone give an accurate local forecast for days ahead. No one could measure simultaneously and with absolute precision the direction and speed of the wind in a turbulent storm on every street corner. We can never know enough about the present to predict future weather with certainty. Yet some would still want to hold that there are not any real gaps in physical processes. It is just a lack of information on our part. A belief that we can in principle predict something, even if we fail in fact, must stem from a prior philosophical position about the way the world works.

The distinction between methodological and metaphysical determinism is relevant, but even the demand that science be determinist in its method can be questioned. Physics has been the main source in recent years of the apparent evidence for indeterminism. This still leaves the philosophical argument of those who see causal explanation as the only tenable form of explanation. For them, real physical gaps and physical indeterminacy may place limitations on scientific understanding, since the alternative has to be randomness. Their view is that random behaviour is meaningless, chance or accidental, because uncaused. It becomes the enemy of scientific understanding. This brings us back to Locke. He was not making the usual distinction between the caused and the random. For him, thinking would be accidental precisely because it was caused by the motion of particles. In other words, the crucial distinction for him was between the rational and the accidental. Thoughts, produced by the behaviour of bits of matter, became not just accidental, but unguided. They possessed no greater sense or wisdom than the blind matter causing them. For Locke, the idea that the juxtaposition of bits of matter could have anything to do with ways to knowledge, let alone with the wisdom of God, seemed self-evidently outrageous. Thought produced by blind, non-rational processes would be equally blind. Yet a determinism that rules out rational explanation as an alternative to causal explanation has to resort to showing that reason is compatible with universal causal explanation. The idea would be that we can all be caused to act as we do, and have reasons for action. We could be caused to have the beliefs we do, and the beliefs could still be rationally grounded. Some philosophers would go so far as to hold that freedom of choice entails determinism, and that unless we think we can rely on a predictable world, and unless our choices can be translated into action through causal mechanisms, we could not be proper agents. This position is much influenced by Hume, but it is unacceptable to those who would see free will as involving, not only the ability to act freely, but the ability to choose freely how to act.

Free will is particularly important for morality, since if we are not free to act one way rather than another, or if our choices are determined, we cannot appear responsible for our actions. We would not then be praiseworthy or blameworthy. At most, the threat of punishment, or the promise of reward, may act as causal factors in manipulating how we behave. The crucial aspect of the debate between determinism and others for our present purposes is how far rational thought is compatible with determinism. If every event has a cause, all my thoughts and beliefs, and indeed any estimate of truth, are equally caused. Yet does not that undermine their validity? It is not enough that we think we are making up our own minds or that we have good reasons for what we say. Our thoughts, and the causes at work on us, may be very far apart. A good example is that of post-hypnotic suggestion. It can be suggested to me under hypnosis that, when I come out of it, I will need to perform some simple, but perhaps unusual, task. I could, for instance, be told that I must get an umbrella and open it inside the building. When this duly happens most people, after hypnosis, will probably give an explanation for what might seem a bizarre act. They might say that they had to check the umbrella because they thought it was broken, or produce some other rationalization. They are in fact giving reasons for an action, the cause of which is very different. They may even be unaware of it. Much neurotic behaviour might be like this, where reasons are given for, say, obsessive hand-washing. The cause may be very different, and is the right subject for psychoanalytic investigation.

The reasons that I give and are at the forefront of my mind are not always sufficient to explain my behaviour. That is why we consider such excuses to be rationalizations and not the real reasons for belief or action. One major difference between reasons and causes is that I must, at some level, be aware of reasons. I do not have to know what is causing me to think or behave in a particular way. The example of rationalization produces the daunting possibility that all our reasons are rationalizations, and that what makes us tick is often far beyond our knowledge or understanding. Reason then becomes the froth at the forefront of our mind. It is not the driving force which makes us who and what we are.

Reasons and Causes

Greek philosophers such as Aristotle thought that rationality is what distinguishes humans from animals. How different are we from animals? We do not normally suppose that a dog weighs up different arguments in an effort to arrive at the truth. It just acts through inherited instinct. Even apes, which can be taught the beginnings of communication through sign language, can hardly be thought to reason in any but the most elementary way. Even then they can only work out means to ends. They may see how to get a banana with a stick, but they certainly cannot be plausibly thought to engage in philosophical thought about the differences between themselves and humans.

Materialists, particularly those imbued with neo-Darwinism, will wish to discount differences between humans and animals as merely ones of degree.

They would see no sharp break between animals and us, claiming that *homo sapiens* is just another animal species with its own peculiar characteristics. We have developed step-by-step from animal ancestry and should still be seen as a kind of animal. This approach, though, seems disingenuous. One of our evolved characteristics is the ability to reason. As a result we are not only able to flourish by adapting to different environments, but are also able to espouse such theories as neo-Darwinism and determinism. Such reasoning appears to aim at truth but, as we saw in chapter 6, evolutionary explanations can often prise the causes of a belief being held away from the issue of its truth.

It is tempting to insist that there be a proper connection between a belief and what it is about. Could we then say that there is a good reason for belief when the belief is caused by the very features in the environment to which it is supposed to refer? Some would produce the example of our ordinary perception of the world to show that there need be no stark opposition between rational and causal explanation. Surely the best reason for believing I am looking at a cat is that there is one in front of me and my eyesight is normal. A neuro-physiological process is begun by the presentation of an object to me and ends with perception and belief. My belief would be a lucky accident if I had not been caused to have it by the presence of the cat.

Correct beliefs, particularly in the case of perception, are the result of causal chains working in a proper way. A belief can be misleading when there is a malfunction in the chain, such as trouble with my eyes. A drug, too, could make me have hallucinations. Any belief would not be well grounded precisely, it seems, because of some intervening cause. My belief would not be the product of 'the right' causal chain. There would be no clear link between me and the objects I believed would be in front of me. It suggests that the reliability of beliefs is a function of the reliability of the mechanisms which produced them. It is only through the proper functioning of my normal senses that I am put in the right relation with the world around me. The issue is, therefore, not causation, but whether it is the right kind of causation. All this seems very mechanistic and is often congenial to naturalists, who wish to integrate their account of how we obtain knowledge with a causal view.

The snag is that talk of the 'proper functioning' of my senses and of the 'reliability' of mechanisms introduces a new dimension. We can see that not all causal histories lead us to true belief. They have themselves to be assessed. The strength of any causal theory is that it links our belief and understanding with the real world. There can be many alternative sets of coherent beliefs.

Those who believe that the earth is flat can make this strange belief fit in with their other beliefs. Beliefs may hang together, but they cannot all be right. There needs, in addition, to be some connection with the real world. Philosophers have often talked of the correspondence of our beliefs with the world, as a way of bringing out the fact that any belief has to be about something. Beliefs must be true in virtue of something in the world. Even though inconsistent beliefs are hardly a sign of truth, coherence alone cannot be a sufficient guarantee.

Causal connections seem to be one way of forging a link between belief and world. The presence of a cat impinges on my retina and triggers a set of neural processes. This may seem reassuring as a basis for my belief. I seem to be connected with the real world because I see the cat. Not all cases are as simple as this. Perceptual mechanisms are very important and they do seem to be triggered by the appropriate stimuli. Thought and language, however, range far more widely than immediate perception. Only empiricists would want to be limited by what we can directly experience. Our reasoning takes over in a way that does not happen, it must be assumed, in the case of animals. The fact that they do not have anything recognizable as a language itself suggests a major difference between them and us.

Philosophy has traditionally linked the power of reason with human freedom and creativity. It is significant that Locke was willing to link words such as 'freedom' and 'choice' with the idea of rational thinking. Reasoned thinking can detach itself from its context and assess its own validity. It is not a knee-jerk response to the environment. Yet this does not combine very easily with contemporary causal accounts. The latter show how we relate to the world and explain how our judgements may be produced. They describe mechanisms. Yet mechanisms can be honed by evolution simply in the interests of survival and reproductive success. Truth may not necessarily coincide with these goals. Are we to suppose, therefore, that human reasoning may not only be fallible, but systematically misleading? If we have reasons for thinking this, we are already relying on our reason. Our ability to criticize and evaluate is an integral part of our ability as rational subjects. We do not just describe how we come to hold certain views. What might be termed a 'normative' element enters in. We do not just have beliefs, but are guided by norms as to what we ought to believe.

Assessing how reliable our beliefs may be can be complicated. It is the major function of epistemology. The idea that we must merely use scientific theory to explain the mechanisms by which we obtain beliefs is to say that epistemology is an illusion. In that case there would be no way of assessing the reliability of beliefs. We would just have them. We would not be able to describe which are better or which are worse. There is then no point in talking of what we ought to believe, rather than just what we do believe. There is not even any way of distinguishing between different kinds of causal chains leading to our beliefs. We may want to say that some are reliable paths to knowledge whilst others are not. This presupposes that we have a grasp of what knowledge is and are able to obtain truth in the first place. It suggests that we can assess what different beliefs are worth, and distinguish between those that happen by luck to be true and those that are properly grounded. This has been a key philosophical task since the time of Socrates and Plato, but it does mean the causes of our beliefs must themselves be rationally assessed. If I catch a train, having looked up an out-of-date timetable, I cannot be said to be acting on reliable information. No doubt, the times are changed annually. Even if the timetable happens still to be right, this is mere chance. What caused my belief was not a good reason for it. Knowing the mechanisms of the production of belief is very different from rationally assessing the grounding of a belief. The quality of the source matters. Animals have beliefs and act on them. They cannot assess how reliable those beliefs are likely to be. They cannot even wonder whether the mechanisms of sight, smell and so on, which give them their information about the external world, are functioning properly.

Philosophy has often insisted on a distinction between the means by which we come to have a belief and the issue of whether the belief is trustworthy, or even true. The means themselves, as we are arguing, have to be assessed. Refusing to do so involves committing what has been called the 'genetic fallacy'. That has been understood as blurring the distinction between the origin of a belief and the question of its truth. A similar point has been made sometimes in the context of science, when the distinction has been drawn between what has been called the 'context of discovery' and the 'context of justification'. What made a scientist come to a certain conclusion, or adopt a particular theory, is a completely different issue from whether it can be proved. Scientists can stumble on important discoveries in all kinds of situations. A blazing row with a colleague might be the spur to a sudden insight. Even insomnia might be. What, though, makes a discovery relevant to other scientists depends on reasons being given which they, for their part, could accept. They do not need to go through the same experiences which brought their colleague his original insight. The latter may have little to do with the truth of the theory in question.

This is why the history of science sometimes diverges from the philosophy of science. The former tries to chart the rather bumpy road which led to scientific advances. Philosophy, on the other hand, is not so interested why one person, or a whole group, came to hold certain beliefs. Individual psychology, and even sociology and economics, might tell us a lot about the development of science. None of them can say anything about why scientific claims might be true. Philosophy wants to provide a rational reconstruction of the development of knowledge, showing how the various steps can be justified. History deals with particular contexts, philosophy with general issues of truth, holding even for people in very different social and historical situations. It may be interesting to find out how Einstein came to believe in the theory of relativity. It is instructive to know of the social and economic conditions that made his work possible. What is perhaps more important, however, is whether scientists can still be justified in accepting it.

Wanting to separate reasons for belief from causes is much the same as trying to separate the social background of belief from its content. In each case, the important point is what is believed and the reasons for believing it. How it came to be believed is a different issue. Causes and reasons can coincide in so far as a certain causal origin may be an indication of truth. I have good reason for believing I see a cow, when I am standing in front of one in good light and have no good grounds for thinking my eyesight is faulty. Even in this simple case, causes are not enough. My reason must tell me that I can rely on the circumstances. It may be reasonable to believe what I do, but the process of rational assessment is never just a causal operation. Philosophy demands that we take nothing for granted.

Do Causes Undermine Reasons?

Those who believe in determinism would resist distinguishing between cause and reason. Just because, by definition, we can never break out of the web of cause and effect, all mental operations must then be explained in causal terms. Reasoning is just a causal mechanism coming in at a higher level, and eventually to be described in neuro-physiological terms. We have quoted E. O. Wilson before, and he pursues materialism relentlessly but consistently. He holds that if thought is reducible to physical processes, it must in principle be predictable. He admits that he must accept that the mind of any particular individual is fundamentally determined and lacking free will. He explains by saying 'If within the interval of a microsecond, the active networks composing the thought were known down to every neuron, molecule and ion, their exact state in the next microsecond might be predicted'.[3] This would, in fact, be operationally impossible, not least because measuring the processes would inevitably interfere with them and alter them. Wilson regards his determinism as irrelevant to ordinary life, and says: 'Because the individual mind cannot be fully known and predicted, the self can go on passionately believing in its own free will'. It can do so, apparently, even though Wilson himself believes that it is false, and wants to persuade the rest of us, too, that it is false. This commitment to free will could even be made consistent with the belief in determinism, since belief in free will, and an instinctive resistance to determinism, could have been built into us by evolution. Wilson takes this line, saying that 'confidence in free will is biologically adaptive'.[4] It is thus in our interests to believe that we are free, even though we are not.

We should be suspicious of all this. How can Wilson himself believe in determinism if it is maladaptive to do so? Is such a belief a biological quirk, soon to be winnowed out, but putting Wilson himself at a disadvantage to the rest of us? Why, then, does he imagine that he can, let alone should, convince us of the truth of determinism? Why should he want us to go against our biological interests? Perhaps he realizes that he is conducting a forlorn campaign, and cannot convince us. Certainly he appears to find it very difficult even to keep to deterministic assumptions himself. If determinism is true, our moral views will themselves be under causal influences of one kind and another. Reason will not be enough to change them, and there would seem little point in moral advocacy. Wilson himself explicitly allows that 'causal explanations of brain activity and evolution, while imperfect, already cover the most facts known about moral behaviour with the greatest accuracy'.[5] Yet some pages later he makes a strong case for the fostering of biological diversity, pleading for what he describes as a 'powerful conservation ethic'.[6] It looks as if he is trying to argue for a moral case, which will influence us. Yet that can only make sense on the assumption that we are free to assess arguments and to take a genuine responsibility for our actions. We would not then be in the grip of physical forces which we may barely comprehend and which we can do nothing about even if we do. We are, it seems after all, at least partly in control of our destiny and that of the biological world around us. We have a moral responsibility, to which Wilson appeals, but which would make no sense at all according to strict determinism. That could only see everything operating ultimately in compliance with the laws of physics and not free moral choices. Wilson himself says that 'moral reasoning will either remain centred on ideas of theology and philosophy, where it is now, or it will shift towards science-based rational analysis'.[7] He wants to do the latter, but fails to see that this makes ordinary reasoning, let alone moral reasoning, impossible.

Where then does this leave a belief in determinism itself? Wilson supposes that we are genetically predisposed to a belief in free will. It must seem odd then that there are any determinists left. Perhaps they have been persuaded by rational argument. That, though, is precisely what determinism cannot allow, since it is then being assumed that reason is an alternative to causation. Some have indeed gone on to say that determinism, and materialism, can never even have been known to be true. This argument was once put forward in pithy form by the scientist, J. B. S. Haldane. He said:

> I am not myself a materialist, because, if materialism is true, it seems to me that we cannot know that it is true. If my opinions are the result of chemical processes going on in my brain, they are determined by the laws of chemistry, not those of logic.[8]

Haldane was later persuaded that this position was mistaken. He retracted what he had earlier maintained, and instead pointed out that opinions are not necessarily misleading just because they are caused by chemical processes. We have seen in the case of perception how causal processes produce true beliefs (assuming that total scepticism is ruled out). The present point, however, is much more subtle. Haldane's original argument was not that caused beliefs must be misleading, but that we could never be in a position to know if they are true or false. Causal processes are equally involved in both truth and falsity. Unless we can distinguish between the two cases, truth becomes a matter of lucky chance. We might be correct and we might not. Wilson suggests that a fervent belief in free will itself has been caused, but is misleading. It is mysterious how he could know this. There seems to be no neutral ground on which he could stand to make the judgement. On determinist assumptions, there could be no undetermined arena in which dispassionate judgements could ever be made about determinism or anything else. This is what makes Haldane's retraction of his original argument unsound. A determinist, or materialist, may well be caused to believe in determinism and be correct. According to determinism, someone might well be programmed to believe in free will and be mistaken. How, given determinism, can this ever be resolved? How could we decide between different sets of causal beliefs, some leading to truth and others leading to falsity? We could not know what is true without the ability to reason about the matter, rather than being arbitrarily caused to believe one thing rather than another.

Determinism, with its close ally materialism, cannot use rational argument with sincerity. Reason, for determinism, must only constitute what a given person at a given time is programmed to think reasonable. We may all be like very sophisticated computers. They can work in full accordance with the laws of logic. Yet they have been programmed to do that and are, in a sense, merely extensions of human minds, and thus designed to work logically. We are thus forced back to the question as to whether our minds or brains have been designed, and if so how. The materialist answer will be that this has happened by evolution through natural selection. Yet we have already seen that this is not a reliable mechanism for arriving at the truth.

The philosopher, Karl Popper, adopts Haldane's original argument and suggests that materialism is incompatible with a reliance on rational argument. He says: 'Materialism may be true, but it is incompatible with rationalism, with the acceptance of the standards of critical argument: for these standards appear from the materialist point of view as an illusion, or at least as an ideology'.[9] Reason assumes the possibility of the free recognition of truth, or of the likelihood of truth. It cannot, in the manner of a tram, however modern, be taken to a predetermined destination by tracks that allow no deviation, whatever the evidence. We might luckily be caused to recognize the evidence as such, but we might not. The determinist thesis can, of course, subside into meaninglessness by simply taking evidence and reasons as causes. Yet if such things are causes, however immaterial, determinism is not saying anything. It normally gains its force through an alliance with a scientific search for causes. A strong determinism can only allow the kind of causes countenanced by naturalist philosophy. Issues of reason and justification must then be ruled out. One cannot in all consistency both believe that all beliefs are caused, even our belief in the truth or falsity of determinism, and still give reasons why people who believe in free will are wrong.

Notes

1   John Locke, *Essay Concerning Human Understanding*, ed. Peter H. Nidditch, Oxford University Press, Oxford, 1975, iv, ch. X, 17, p. 627.
2   David Hume, *An Enquiry Concerning Human Understanding*, section viii, part 2, ed. E. Steinberg, Hackett, Indianapolis, 1993, p. 61.
3   E. O. Wilson, *Consilience*, Alfred A. Knopf, New York, 1998, p. 120.

4   Ibid.
5   Ibid., p. 241.
6   Ibid., p. 292.
7   Ibid., p. 240.
8   J. B. S. Haldane, 'I Repent an Error', *Literary Guide*, April 1954, p. 7.
9   Karl Popper, *The Self and its Brain*, Springer International, Berlin, 1977, p. 81.

8

Materialism and the Laws of Nature

The Status of Mathematics

Determinism is a philosophical thesis. Science must face the possibility that whatever irregularities it uncovers, there is always the chance that we are living in a pool of order in the midst of a sea of disorder. The universe stretches far beyond our reach in time and space. We can never even be sure that we are living in a typical region. Perhaps, too, as Kant would have us believe, our understanding of the world is as much the result of the nature of the human mind, and the categories it works with, as the character of reality itself. Perhaps the apparent order of the world is in the eye of the beholder. The idea that we live in a world that is independently ordered, and in such a way that we can understand it, may seem to be little short of a miracle. Perhaps for that reason it has to be discarded. As we have seen, even appeals to evolutionary explanations are of little help, since they themselves presuppose the theory of evolution, and the fact that it applies to the physical world. That merely begs the question.

Determinism overreaches itself, as a thesis. Even if it is true, it is impossible to argue for it rationally, since it undermines the possibility of rational argument. Yet does this failure itself cast any doubt on the alleged orderliness and regularity of the physical processes that go to make up the world? Much faith has always been placed in the supposed uniformity of nature. Blanket determinism may undermine science itself as a rational pursuit. Scientists must still assume some kind of order in the world for scientific research to be possible in the first place. At the same time, an absolutely ordered universe would make science impossible. Scientists would be manipulated into holding theories by whatever causal influences were paramount.

One problem facing any determinist theory is just which set of causes to emphasize. Those who talk of the social construction of science would stress social ones. Some would prefer explanation in terms of genes, and others in terms of neurons. All these may be made compatible, if everything is thought reducible to the laws of physics. Yet many theorists, such as sociologists, would feel that important parts of their explanations had been missed out if everything was put in those terms. We can postpone wider questions about reduction and concentrate on the issue of the laws of physics. Some would regard these as encapsulating the ultimate explanation for everything. They are naturally linked to the issue of determinism, since they have often been thought to provide the essential framework for the working of the physical world. In vivid contrast to arguments about the historical trajectory of evolution, they have often been seen not so much as summaries of what has happened in the past, but as prescriptions for what has to happen. Biology has never thought that particular species have to come into existence or be wiped out. These things just occur because of various environmental pressures. Physics, however, has not looked at the history of the universe. Like philosophy, it has wanted to find the reality underlying various appearances.

The very distinction between reality and appearance, the stable, eternal world of laws and their various changing manifestations, is reminiscent of a Platonic philosophical framework. Plato's distinction between two worlds may have led to theological views about a distinction between an eternal, unchanging God, and the familiar world of change and decay. His world of Forms was populated, however, by impersonal standards of mathematical perfection and moral perfection, including, above all, Goodness. He was strongly influenced by the Pythagorean stress on the importance of number in the constitution of the world. Disputes between materialists and proponents of a two-world view can appear in unexpected places. Even nowadays it is not just a question of those who make a distinction between body and mind, or world and spirit. Others make a fundamental distinction between the absolute, necessary framework in which the development of the physical world takes place, and the contingent events within it. There is the same dualist pattern of argument at work. There is the same contrast between apparently haphazard events in the physical world, and something else, eternal and untouched by change. We have in that case to see the physical world, in true Platonic style, as copying rigid and absolute exemplars. In this instance, however, the real world is not thought to be a spiritual one, or a heaven in the presence of God. It is a much more abstract place, perhaps indeed more like Plato's own conception of the Forms. It is a mathematical world, containing all the certainties of mathematics. The standards according to which the physical world operates then exist in some form apart from the physical world. This conception is bound to be an assault on materialism, since the existence of such abstract standards cannot be given any material expression. If we wish to measure this world against something beyond itself, that suggests that the physical world is not all that there is.

Questions about the role of mathematics are central to any philosophical understanding of the nature of the world and of our place in it. Mathematics is an instrument of the human mind and is apparently constructed by human beings. At the same time, it appears to bear an intimate relation to the workings of the physical universe. The whole point about so-called laws of nature is that they must become 'compressible'. As the physicist John Barrow puts it, in talking of ordered patterns: 'If it is possible to store the information in an abbreviated form shorter than the sequence itself, then the sequence is disregarded as non-random and we call it compressible'.[1] An arbitrary generalization that cannot be expressed in mathematical terms is of no use to physics. Yet why should one be able to match up understanding with reality in such a precise way? It is possible to define the idea of the random as what is incompressible in mathematical terms. What is ordered is what is compressible. Science's search for regularities is never a search for coincidences and temporary alignments. It is the search for deep patterns in nature, and mathematics forms the collection of all possible patterns. It is therefore concerned not just with what happens to be the case but with what could be so. Much energy in physics is spent on looking for basic patterns which can form a unified theory, bringing all the various parts of science together. This search for unification has long been a goal. Newton, for example, was able to provide a theory unifying celestial and terrestrial gravitation.

There is a clear link between the idea of mathematical compressibility, reflecting patterns in the physical world, and the idea of intelligibility. This appears to draw together in a graphic manner the nature of the real world and our ability to understand it. What is the relation of the real world, mathematical 'objects', and the human mind? Many mathematicians are themselves realists about mathematics in a consciously Platonic fashion. They do not think that mathematics is about physical objects, whether as simple as apples or pears, or as complicated as the subject matter of physics. Mathematical truths, it seems, are independent of the human mind, as well as being separate from the physical world. They are discovered, not invented.

An alternative position would be a 'constructivism' about mathematics, that treats mathematical objects as purely the product of human minds, not existing independently. The argument is reminiscent of similar disagreements in other areas of human understanding. The difference is that, for the mathematical realist, the objects in question are distinct from physical ones. Two apples and two apples may make four apples, but the numbers two and four, and their properties, are regarded as being totally different. The fact that twice two is four is then neither a projection by the human mind, nor an implicit description of physical objects. It is an abstract truth, existing separately and holding universally. Some mathematicians will be ready to treat this abstract world as every bit as real as the one containing apples and pears.

Mathematics and Materialism

Materialists would take great exception to all this. They would not look kindly on abstract objects of any kind, and let alone those with such an obvious Platonic pedigree. Just because the shadow of Plato falls over so much modern philosophy, his philosophical position, and particularly the dualism inherent in it, provides a ready target for those who wish to put forward the type of materialist position he explicitly attacked. Among these is the contemporary French neurobiologist Jean-Pierre Changeux, who wants to say that mathematical objects exist materially in people's brains. He says:

> *Our brain is a complex physical object. As such, it constructs 'representations' corresponding to physical states. In the head of a mathematician, mathematical objects are material objects - 'mental objects' if you like - with properties that are analysable by a reflex process . . . these mathematical objects correspond to physical states of our brain in such a way that it ought in principle to be possible to observe them from the outside looking in, using various methods of brain imaging.*[2]

He makes an implicit reference to evolution when he suggests that our cerebral faculties of reasoning and logic are linked to the way the brain is organized, and existed, at least in part, even in *homo erectus*, a tool maker. Yet this is not a scientific theory, even though put forward by a scientist. It is a classic philosophical position of a somewhat crude sort. The idea that we can observe mathematical objects in the brain follows from the materialist identity between brain states and mental operations. Yet, if there is a correlation between thinking mathematically and certain forms of brain activity, it seems hard to identify the two. How can complicated equations be the same as the activity of neural networks? If an analogy with computers is sought, the results of their working still have to be interpreted and understood by humans. Changeux, however, is determined not to allow mathematics to float free of any physical realization, so that it could form part of some metaphysical world, parallel to and distinct from the world we inhabit. The way in which he quickly moves from the idea of a representation to that of a physical state, and from material objects to physical objects, shows that a strong doctrine of the priority of the physical is at work. He assumes that referring to anything else must be empty. Not just mental operations, but what they are supposed to be about, have to be mere physical events.

One of the most problematic features of the mind is the way in which it can be apparently directed at different states of affairs, whether imaginary or real. The 'aboutness' of mental operations has sometimes been thought to be the characteristic badge of the mental. This is always difficult to capture in any materialist interpretation of the mental. When I think, I think of something. When I am angry, I am angry at somebody. When I reason, I reason about things. The question of the so-called 'intentionality' of the mind is an important feature. This means that the mind is aiming itself at something like an arrow at a target. Bits of stuff, like brains, do not at first sight appear to have this characteristic. Needless to say, this is a classic difficulty for materialism, which has to rely exclusively on causal accounts. Any simple reduction of mathematics to events in the brain does not seem to be able to cope with the simple question how we can think about things, especially when they appear to be abstract. Mathematicians and neurobiologists seem to be in significantly different lines of business. Mathematics is certainly not primarily about states in the brain.

Materialism, in fact, has a general difficulty about the status of thinking and its connection with brain processes. It has a particular difficulty in coping with thought about abstract objects. The use of the term 'object' ought perhaps to alert us to a common temptation, highlighted by the later work of Wittgenstein. Language does not always function in the same way, he warned us. Just because some language refers to physical objects, such as houses, it does not follow that all words stand for 'things'. He was particularly concerned with the use of the word 'pain' to refer to what might seem to be a 'mental object'. The point is that non-physical 'objects' of thought and experience should not necessarily be thought to be like physical ones, only different. We should be aware of the context in which words are used.

Meaning is intimately associated with use, and we should not think that all words are labels for 'things'. Mathematical objects are not necessarily ghostly surrogates for physical ones. Just because a word appears to be about something, it does not mean that there is a thing, whether real or imaginary, concrete or abstract, that the word is about. Platonism often seems fond of supposing that there are real objects for general terms to be about, whether terms such as 'goodness' and 'justice' or more mathematical ones. Whatever the reasons for this, we should not too easily imagine that all language gets its meaning through naming things, rather than through being embedded in a particular context and obtaining its meaning from that.

This general warning is well taken. It does not automatically follow that because we talk about, say, the number seven, that it exists in some special realm. Yet we can all talk about the same number, and proofs can be given about it that are valid for everyone. It is more than the product of a particular brain process. Mathematicians often talk of a sense of discovery, or a flash of intuition, about some difficult proof. They may suddenly see how to solve it, even though the process of working out to prove it for the benefit of other mathematicians may take many days. One mathematician, in argument with Changeux, describes how 'one has the impression of exploring a world step-by-step - and of connecting up the steps so well, so coherently, that one knows it has been entirely explored'.[3] His reaction is that it is impossible not to 'feel that such a world has an independent existence'.

The actual status of the truth as described in mathematics will be much contested. Basic philosophical positions are at stake. Materialists are in fact bound to be somewhat embarrassed. Their campaign to insist on the sole reality of physical objects appears to founder at the very beginning with the assumptions necessary for the conduct of physics itself. Physics depends on mathematics, and it is at least arguable that the abstract concepts necessary for mathematics cannot themselves be given a physical explanation. Even if the Platonist interpretation is rejected, and mathematics is viewed as a cultural product, a social construction, there are difficulties for the materialist in saying what this would amount to in physical terms. Social meanings seem very different from bits of stuff.

Changeux, himself, wants to talk of mathematical objects as cultural objects, or, as he puts it as well, as 'public representations of mental objects'.[4] He regards these as being the products of brains, being 'propagated' from one brain to another. This kind of language is widely used. It involves not one, but several dubious steps. There is, firstly, the step from brain to mind, from physical process to actual understanding. Then there is the idea of a representation, of something 'standing for' something else. That itself appears to be an abstract, non-material, idea. In addition, there is the difficulty of understanding culture itself, and what cultural objects are, in physicalist terms. The way of doing so is to translate them into terms acceptable to neurophysiology. Yet it is at least questionable whether culture, itself the realm of meaning and significance, can be grouped with what Locke might term 'blind' physical processes. We must also reckon with the step from the level of the public and social to that of the individual. We may share a culture, but it is not clear in what sense we can share brain processes, even though words like 'propagation' are used. When people talk of 'memes' as units of culture, passed on by analogy with genes, they can be talking of such things as religious beliefs, or a taste for the music of Bach. These have to be determined by non-physical criteria. Even if a correlation were discovered between bits of culture and storage in particular brain structures, it would still be difficult to think that the shared beliefs could be explained in neural terms. Hearing a sublime piece of music cannot easily be reduced to the mere reception of sound waves, even though it may involve that.

A materialist will typically be a realist about the physical world. The whole point of materialism is to hold that the only genuine reality is what is physical, existing independent of our conceptions of it. Our concepts themselves do not just have to be realized in physical form. They must themselves actually be physical. Yet this is very hard to make plausible, since ideas of reason, justification and evidence can have no place. The idea of an argument in favour of materialism is decidedly shaky. What is an argument in material form? It may be a series of neurons firing, but there could be little reason for us to prefer one set of neurons firing to another. Opposition to materialism must, if materialism is correct, be just a series of physical events. How then can one prefer, let alone argue for, one series rather than another?

Laws of Nature

The more the materialist analyses mental and cultural events into physical processes, the more it appears that such processes have patterns. The physical world has to be orderly and regular. Indeed, we have already encountered the point that we could not have evolved in a disorderly world. Yet a material stress on the causal order of the physical world raises again the question of the status of so-called 'laws of nature'. Can they be properly understood within a materialist framework? There can certainly be causal regularities in the world, but many philosophers from Hume on, have been reluctant to see them as in any sense necessary. A Platonic conception of eternal laws, understood mathematically, may incline us to see them as necessarily true. They would then contrast with the world around us, which is constantly changing. This can give ammunition to determinism, but it is paradoxical that relying on fixed laws of nature, governing everything, may be congenial to materialism and yet strike at its very roots. The latter can take note of apparent patterns in nature, but believing in their necessity is another matter. It suggests that the material world is subject to constraints that, it seems, can only come from beyond the structure of physical things.

Contemporary physicists are quite ready to see physical laws as themselves contingent. If they were metaphysically necessary, that would mean that they have to be true not only across the known universe, but 'in all possible worlds'. Philosophers often talk of truth in all possible worlds to stress that certain things are logically necessary. They could not be different, unless we were to find ourselves in a mesh of contradictions. Two and two could never equal five in any surroundings. Mathematical truths, in fact, come in precisely this category, as would the basic laws of logic, such as the law of non-contradiction. There is no world where an animal could simultaneously be both a dog and not a dog. There might well be worlds where there are no dogs, and indeed no animals. The fact that they existed would not be logically necessary.

Seeing physical laws in this way, as part of the fabric of a world which could be very different, is to see them in a very different light from those who have betrayed them as fixed and unchanging. No doubt we could not live in this world if it were very different physically, and there could be many worlds without creatures like us. That is to say that certain conditions are physically necessary for existence, and for the existence of a world like ours. That is different from metaphysical necessity. Our world does not have to exist with its familiar constituents. None of us has to, and indeed one day will not. We, and our whole world, are contingent. Similarly, water could not be water if it was not composed of hydrogen and oxygen. Those elements are essential to it being what it is. That does not mean that water has to exist, or that very different liquids may not exist in different worlds.

Physical laws can be seen as bound up with the conditions that obtained at the beginning of our universe. With different conditions there would have been different laws and a different kind of physical universe. The physical necessities obtaining in our universe are not logically necessary. Other possibilities could arise. If, though, there is only one possible unified theory of physics, that might seem to place a limit on what could count as a physical law. We are then back with a Platonist picture of such laws being necessary in a metaphysical sense. Once it is accepted that there could be radically different universes operating according to different systems of physical laws, the idea of one mathematically necessary theory has to give way to a different conception of law. Even if we are not attracted by the idea of many universes, and see no reason for positing them, that is not the same as saying that they are metaphysically impossible. Nevertheless, we should be on our guard of thinking that a real possibility is something that actually does exist in some shadowy realm. A possible world is not a funny kind of real world. It is merely possible. A possibility is what it claims to be, something that could happen but may not. It need not actually exist at all.

Why has the universe taken the form it has, if there was no metaphysical necessity for it to do so? Why has the world developed in such a way that we can understand it with the aid of the mathematical tools at human disposal? The question of the origin of order and regularity has to return to centre stage, as a philosophical question that cannot be brushed aside. Once the contingency of physical laws is fully accepted, things could obviously have been very different. Conditions supporting life could have been very much more complex, so complex that our mathematics could not capture its complexity. We would not be able to understand it. Yet we do appear to understand a surprisingly large amount, and it is one of the tasks of philosophy to explain why this is possible. Philosophers may be tempted to avoid this kind of metaphysical question because they prefer to limit themselves to ones that they have some idea of how to answer. This can be very stultifying, and philosophy can become restricted to more and more mundane matters. This is no doubt a prime motive for the 'scientism' of some philosophers, and the relativism of others. The former can shelter behind science, oblivious of the fact that it has to make large philosophical assumptions to get started. The latter are content to restrict themselves to what people happen to think in different social backgrounds. The fact remains, however, that the mathematical compressibility of the physical world is left unexplained. No philosopher should be content to accept it at face value. It is what makes physics possible, and enters into the foundations of our empirical knowledge.

Once laws are seen not as the enduring constraints of any physical world, but just as the way our universe happens to be organized, a further problem arises. We have several times mentioned that such laws are descriptive, not prescriptive. They may tell us of the conditions under which the physical world normally operates. There should be no indication that everything has to be like this. At best, laws describe the regularities and patterns which happen to hold. They pick out tendencies and propensities in the way that various bits of matter behave. It is easy to fall into talking of how laws cannot be broken, and to suggest that physical laws actually determine what should happen. Indeed, such a picture follows naturally from the picture of an iron-clad necessity, dictating an invariant and eternal set of conditions. Laws are not the source of the regularities that undoubtedly subsist in the physical world. They are summaries of them.

Contingent Order

Suggesting that laws may not be necessary does not detract from a realist understanding of the physical world. The world exists in its own right, with its own processes and structures, however we comprehend it. That does not mean that we should uphold a Platonic idea that the patterns displayed in these processes are themselves somehow copies of some eternal realm. The law-like relationships we may uncover reflect the real powers of entities in the physical world. They are not artefacts of human understanding. That is partly why there is such an issue about how and why the human mind is so fitted to understand them. Nevertheless, the 'laws' that are articulated to account for the order inherent in nature are the products of the human mind. They are models which approximate to nature and to some extent treat it as if it were in an ideal state. A very simple example is the law that water boils at a hundred degrees centigrade. It does at sea level, but altitude alters the situation. Very often descriptions of apparently unalterable laws actually refer to an idealized situation which may often not hold in the ordinary world. While it is wrong to think of science as being in the business of construction rather than discovery, the human mind does play an active role in trying to make sense of all the information flooding in from outside.

Karl Popper points out that 'there is no road, royal or otherwise, which leads of necessity from a "given" set of specific facts to any universal law'.[5] He famously saw such laws as hypotheses or conjectures, subject to trial and possible elimination in the light of experience. In other words, he was looking for what might make a theory false, rather than what might make it true. As a result, he felt that no scientific theory was ever certain. It was always open to future criticism, review and even falsification. This is probably to take up too agnostic a position about the possibility of scientific knowledge, and indeed about the powers of the human mind. Openness to criticism is certainly, as we have seen, a philosophical virtue, and a valuable method of sorting out truth from falsity. If, however, we are always looking for how we might be mistaken, without any assurance that we could be right, we could easily end in despair.

The Enlightenment conception of human reason may have been too optimistic about our capabilities. Our fallibility and limitations of perspective are all too obvious. That should not mean that we become too pessimistic about human rationality. Just because we may not be able to know everything, does not of itself mean that we can know nothing. Yet human science cannot shake off its tentative and provisional nature. The mere fact that the regularities described by physical laws are contingent, makes it obvious that the laws cannot contain within themselves any explanation as to why they hold. In the realm of necessary truth, mathematics may provide its own explanation, since what is necessary has to be the case. Physical laws are not in this position.

This conditional and provisional status of laws does pose further philosophical problems. The main conclusion is that they should be seen as having an epistemological and not a metaphysical status. Laws are to be seen as the outcome of relating regularities, which we have discovered in nature. They are not necessarily part of a fixed physical state. Some philosophical views, such as those of Spinoza, have historically seen the 'universal laws of nature' as divine decrees, following necessarily from the nature of God. This, though, is to make far too close an identification between God and the world. If there is a God who created the physical world, there is no reason to suppose that God had to create it in one way rather than another. That would limit God's freedom and God's power. If there is no God, there is no reason to suppose that the world has to have one nature rather than another. The very idea of contingency suggests that we must ourselves discover how the world works, just because it does not have to have one particular set of laws. Physics may rely on mathematics, but it is also an empirical science. It is not enough to see what holds mathematically in order to understand the world. We have to see what actually happens. That is why the methods of philosophy are insufficient for science. Only observation and experiment can show us the particular nature of the world we live in.

'Natural philosophy', as it used to be called, has developed into different sciences, which understand the need for contact with a contingent world. We cannot just use pure thought about what ought to be so. Yet the reasons for this must themselves be philosophical. Experience and investigation would be superfluous, unless we were situated in a changing world, which does not necessarily behave in a particular way. Contingency is not the whole story. There has to be order present, which stops the physical world being one of chaos and randomness. This order is symbolized by the Greek word 'cosmos', which carries with it the idea of arrangement and is also the root of the word 'cosmetic'. Contingency stops science becoming like pure mathematics, exploring the realm of necessary truth. Without the additional fact of order, science would not be able to make the generalizations and predictions to which it is accustomed. It must be able to assume that the part of the word it examines is representative of other parts elsewhere and at other times.

The idea of contingent order is, from the philosophical point of view, a precondition for the possibility of science. There may still be a question of why the world does happen to be ordered. That has been the traditional cue in philosophy for introducing an argument from design to the existence of God. Those who wish to resist this move may say that it is a 'brute fact' incapable of further explanation that the world behaves in a regular and ordered fashion. Alternatively, as we have seen, they can exploit the idea of many universes to show that it is a matter of chance that one of them has been able to produce life. Whichever way is chosen, the one path that is self-defeating is simply to deny the fact of order and regularity in the world. That would be to undermine the assumptions on which science has to be based.

Talk of laws reflects our attempt to understand, even from a limited and partial perspective, the processes which constitute the physical universe. This does not mean, though, that we should believe in determinism or in rigid causal laws. Tendencies, propensities and regularities are not the same as any form of necessity. The very fact of contingency means that whatever happens does not have to, and other things could happen. The laws we put forward do not fully reflect the actual workings of the physical world, which may be considerably less rigid than has sometimes been assumed.

Naturalism wants to talk of the self-sufficiency of natural processes, and the closure of the physical domain. This suggests boundaries, which are difficult to mark out. Causal closure is none too clear a notion when we realize we are confronted with the whole of reality, which could be infinite. When scientists conduct experiments, artificial limitations can be placed, so that what is being tested is being examined within defined boundaries. Influences beyond these boundaries will be screened out, if possible. That is why experiments are often hard to set up, difficult to reproduce, and not always representative of the real world. In the ordinary physical world, there is no such artificial closure. There is no self-contained, physical system. Whatever physical area we are looking at, even if it is a whole tract of the universe, there is always likely to be something beyond it, perhaps influencing it.

The physicalist will retort that whatever is beyond is, nevertheless, physical, operating according to the same laws. This, though, is to fall into the same trap of viewing laws as part of reality, as having an ontological status. If, however, they are seen as epistemological, merely as part of the way we organize our understanding of physical reality, we can make generalizations of what is likely to happen. That is very far from the metaphysical, or ontological, thesis of determinism. It is far short of a justification for asserting the causal closure of the physical world, with clearly demarcated boundaries.

Reference to causal closure may owe more to a doctrine of physicalism than of determinism. Its point may not be that laws capture the whole of the nature of physical reality. The claim may be that only the physical world can have a causal effect. Only physical causes can then be causes. Nothing that happens within the physical domain can be explained in terms of anything non-physical. This depends for its clarity on a transparent definition of what it is to be physical, and the object of scientific investigation. This suggests that what is at issue is not just what happens in remote corners of the universe. We are brought right back home, since at stake is our own nature as human beings. Are we merely physical creatures, controlled by our physical brain? Are our minds and their contents to be viewed as somehow part of the physical world, if they are to have any effect? In the end, the fiercest battles about naturalism do not concern the nature of the physical world, or how we can come to know it. They concern our own character as reasoning beings, and the properties of the human mind.

Notes

1 John Barrow, *Pi in the Sky*, Oxford University Press, Oxford, 1992, p. 163.
2 Jean-Pierre Changeux and Alain Connes, *Conversations on Mind, Matter and Mathematics*, Princeton University Press, Princeton, NJ, 1995, p. 14.
3 Ibid., p. 30.
4 Ibid., p. 35.
5 Karl Popper, *Objective Knowledge*, Oxford University Press, Oxford, 1972, p. 359.

9

The Brain and the Mind

The Attack on Dualism

Nowhere are issues about materialism more keenly fought than in discussions about the nature of the human mind. This is hardly surprising, as our own self-evaluation is at stake. Are we mere machines, can we be distinguished from animals in any important respect, or are we perhaps in possession of unique faculties that set us totally apart? We have already seen how Socrates and Plato reacted against the materialism of some of their contemporaries. For them, as for Aristotle, the question of purpose was paramount. It was not, they all thought, just a question of what matter they were made of, or what causes had produced certain events. A system of mechanistic causes could never deal with questions about the reasons why an action was undertaken, or the purpose for which it was performed. Reference to causes are backward looking, concentrating on what produced something. There is never any question of their encompassing purpose or reason.

The inability of materialist philosophy to cope with questions of rationality has always been its weakness. It cannot account for why we ought to believe or choose something. Epistemological norms are ruled out in favour of descriptive causes. Yet when reason is put in question, so must be the nature of what might be termed the 'rational subject'. What is the 'I' that apparently chooses what to believe or what to do? As we have seen, when reason is questioned, so is freedom, which we need in order to reason, and so are wider issues of personal responsibility. The very idea of a person as an agent becomes much more problematic.

Since the seventeenth century, the 'dualism' between mind and body, championed by Descartes, has been much discussed. This radical separation of the two, treating them as separate 'things', might even be dignified by the term 'common sense', but it raises difficult questions about their interaction. Our brain is very closely connected with the kind of persons we are. The effect of alcohol or drugs on the brain can result in a major alteration of mental states. Brain damage, however caused, can also have a profound and often permanent impact on an individual. Physical ageing processes can involve a tragic mental deterioration. At the same time, the brain needs stimulation, and particularly at a young age, the right kind of stimulation can reinforce the building of neural connections and the increase of mental capacity. The kind of jobs we have can alter the neural configuration of the brain. Even the brains of London taxi drivers have been shown to have developed in specific ways, as a consequence of the rigorous training they receive in the knowledge of London geography and street patterns. Such examples can be multiplied, as understanding of the role of different regions of the brain increases. The mind can never be seen as something existing in a totally different realm, only interacting with the brain when necessary. The two appear to be linked so closely that many would say that they are indissoluble. The question then arises whether they can even be thought of as two 'things' interacting with each other.

Gilbert Ryle, one of the most influential Oxford philosophers of the twentieth century, is famous for dismissing the mind as 'the ghost in the machine'. This was a consequence of the way in which he treated linguistic references to mental states as being in fact about tendencies, or dispositions, to behave in particular ways. He is often regarded as a 'behaviourist' who stressed the centrality of public behaviour rather than private experience. However that may be, if a mind is a ghostly (and presumably non-existent) entity, that may suggest that, once it is discarded, all we are left with is a machine. Yet, in that case, who are 'we'? This last point is crucial. Once mental contents are reduced to brain processes, we appear to be left with a multiplicity of parallel brain events. There is then the question as to what, if any, unifying factor there is, beyond the obvious one of them all happening to be taking place in the same physical environment.

Am 'I', therefore, to be dissolved into various patterns of physical events in the brain? Certainly 'dualism' meets unremitting scorn from many scientists and philosophers. It is taken as obvious that the mind is not a thing or substance, and that 'I' have no substantial existence either. This use of the term 'substance' is deliberate in that, in philosophical parlance, a substance has not necessarily been thought material. The important point, from the time of Aristotle, is that it has been the subject of properties, and therefore an entity in its own right. That is why 'substance dualism', according to which the mind is thought to be independent of the body, is distinct from 'property dualism'. In the latter a physical entity, such as the brain, might be thought to acquire non-physical properties. There would then be different kinds of properties, but not different kinds of things having those properties.

Needless to say, both forms of dualism would be ruled out by physicalists. One of them, Paul M. Churchland, writes: 'The religious hypothesis of mind-body dualism has been in deep trouble with evolutionary biology, and with several other sciences as well, for more than a century. It didn't need any special input from artificial intelligence or neuro-science to make it scientifically implausible.'[1]

Questions about the mind and the body no doubt have religious implications, not least because it is important for Christianity, as well as other religions, to be able to show that the idea of our personal survival after death is not logically impossible. Yet it is crucial to realize that the issue is still a strictly philosophical one, and dualism and its competitors have to stand or fall on philosophical grounds alone. It is no use making up one's mind about such issues on the basis of what one hopes is true, whether from the perspective of theism or atheism. Churchland himself appears to squeeze philosophy out of the picture by appealing only to scientific evidence. This is perhaps paradoxical, as he is himself a philosopher. Whatever the scientific evidence, there will always remain a question not just what is evidence for, but also how it is interpreted within a more general framework. Questions about the significance of scientific findings cannot avoid becoming philosophical. The idea that fundamental explanations about the mind are a problem solely for empirical science only makes sense if materialism is true. If everything that can be sensibly said about the mind can be translated without loss of meaning to descriptions of states of the brain, it follows that the empirical investigation of the latter would tell us all we really need to know. That is a large philosophical assumption, and it has to come at the end of an argument, not the beginning.

E. O. Wilson himself rules out philosophy as the means of talking about the relation of mind and brain. He holds that 'Belief in the intrinsic unity of knowledge . . . rides ultimately on the hypothesis that every mental process has a physical grounding, and is consistent with the natural sciences'.[2] Wilson buttresses his position by saying that 'virtually all contemporary scientists and philosophers, expert on the subject, agree that the mind, which comprises consciousness and rational process, is the brain at work'. This type of grand statement is no substitute for philosophical argument. Counting heads is never relevant for the question of truth. Most people, even experts, can be, and often are, wrong. Dualism, as such, is undeniably unfashionable, but in recent years eminent scientists and philosophers have championed it. Wilson, however, covers himself. However apparently eminent and respected they may be, if they do not reduce the mind to the brain in classic materialist fashion, that itself proves for Wilson that they are not expert on the subject.

Why is dualism so unfashionable, particularly when it seems to represent the ordinary opinion of the average person? There is always an appreciable time-lag of at least a generation between the adoption of a particular philosophical consensus and its effect on people outside the profession. No doubt there is an even greater time-lag before the absorption into common sense of the views of a cross-disciplinary intellectual consensus. Are we to assume that gradually our human self-understanding will be altered, so we cease thinking of our reason and our minds as in any way distinct from our bodies? It is hard to overestimate the repercussions of such a change of belief.

Are We Machines?

One area where this matters is not so much the question of the blurring of the distinction between humans and animals. It is, rather, the question of how far humans can continue to be regarded as in any way less machine-like than 'real' machines. Computer power is increasing by leaps and bounds, so that one may suppose that, with the increase in their complexity, they will even surpass humans in intellectual capacity, certainly in such areas as memory and an ability to learn from it. A computer can already beat a chess champion. Chess is, of course, a rule-governed activity, and a computer's power of analysis is especially suited to doing well in it. Whether the computers can excel in more creative activities is another matter. Could they determine which ends are worth pursuing, as opposed to how to reach prescribed ends? Answers to questions like these will be influenced by which philosophical position one holds. A physicalist would be confident that any facet of the human brain can be replicated by machinery. As a consequence, computers, or even robots, may be at least the equal of people in any intellectual capacity. It is even suggested that, by means of non-invasive scanning technology in the future, a person's brain may be scanned and their mind down-loaded to a computer. The question that can then be asked is, in the words of one enthusiast for so-called 'spiritual machines',[3] whether the 'person' who emerges in the machine is the same consciousness as the person who was scanned. The mere fact that the question can be asked shows the way in which physicalist assumptions have taken over. What is the connection between brain processes, however copied, and consciousness, let alone the nature of a person? The gap between what is seen to be going on in my brain by various imaging techniques, and what I am conscious of, is not a gap that can be simply closed by more complex technology. A great deal of philosophical argument is necessary to show that there is even a very close connection between the two realms.

We are all liable to be overawed by the impressive power of computers and their increasing control over our everyday activities. The more complex they become, indeed, the more it seems possible that we can lose control over their activities. Learning processes mean that computers can become 'smarter', using self-organizing methods. Speech recognition systems are a case in point, and they are rapidly becoming a part of our ordinary lives. Yet however complicated, computers are still tools, used as extensions of the human mind. They depend on programming and on human purposes and interests. The fact that so many people are willing to see a blurring of any gap between humans and machines is itself indicative of a basic philosophical outlook.

We have, in the course of this book, often come upon the comparison of people with machines, whether the clockwork ones of the eighteenth century or the computers of the twenty-first. Yet if people are merely machines, why should not machines be regarded as people? Perhaps they should even be regarded as having rights. The fact that such things are being seriously said might suggest that there is something very wrong with the initial assumptions. The idea of a machine suggests something designed for a purpose, as computers undoubtedly are. That is precisely not what a materialist is trying to say.

One aspect of the notion that increasing complexity in computers makes them take on human characteristics is the idea that mind is not separable from the brain, but in some sense emerges from it. When a certain level of neural complexity is reached, it is thought that the mind will inevitably produce consciousness. This position is not as transparent as it appears. On one side there are those philosophers who refuse to accept that being conscious is different from having neural processes occurring in the brain. This is a radical view, which follows clearly enough from materialism. Thoughts and feelings to which I alone have access do not seem to fit very well into a scientific view of the world. As a result many are contemptuous of the so-called 'folk psychology' employed by us all to describe our inner lives. We should not, it seems, rest content with our ordinary understanding of conscious states, in what Dennett dismisses as the 'Cartesian Theatre'. There is, he would say, no mystery in the fact of consciousness, no inner world with its own characteristic nature. The apparent phenomena of consciousness are really, he would claim, 'all physical effects of the brain's activities'.[4] Other 'eliminative materialists', such as Paul Churchland, would also dismiss the content of minds, and think that descriptions and explanations of 'mental' events must be on terms acceptable to science. They must be restricted to publicly observable phenomena, presumably connected with neural activation. For instance, he talks of the similar taste of apricot and peaches, and says: 'The subjective taste just is the activation pattern across the four types of tongue receptors, as represented downstream in one's taste cortex'.[5] He points out that the peach pattern is very similar to the apricot one.

Even talking of observable phenomena highlights a difficulty. 'Phenomena' are called such from the Greek for 'things appearing' to someone. There is still a tacit reference to the mind and how things look. There are strictly no appearances without minds to register them. Science itself depends on the systematization of experience. There must be subjects of conscious experience for science to exist in the first place. This may yet all be explained in terms of physical processes, but it is remarkably difficult to get minds entirely out of the picture. The ambition of some, however, is to show how our experiences are not merely caused by brain processes, or correlated with them. Somehow they are those neural events.

The assertion of the identity of mind and brain has been a consistent theme of some philosophers for over a generation. Yet identity can work in either direction. Why should we not say that all brain events are really mental? That would be an idealist position and is the opposite of materialism. It is all too easy to smuggle materialist assumptions, by assuming that talk of identity is itself to talk of the brain. This kind of view has become more sophisticated, and it is now often recognized that the same mental event could occur with different physical processes, just as the same computer software could be run on different kinds of hardware. This has become known as 'functionalism'. A mental event is regarded as having no intrinsic qualities, or separate existence, but is just what relates certain inputs to the brain and subsequent outputs. Its status arises from the job it performs, and not what it is in itself. A parallel example is that an artificial heart could perform the same function as a natural one. Its function, though, is not something separate from the heart.

This doctrine that mental occurrences are merely part of a 'black box', linking external stimuli to responses by the organism, can be given in different versions. Ultimately, though, the message is bound to be the same. How things 'look' to us, how they 'feel', and what we are conscious of, is not the central part of the story to be told. Pain, for example, is not to be defined in terms of feelings we introspect. Our inner life is not a private stage which we alone can view. The nature of pain has to be understood in terms that do not appeal to consciousness at all, just as the special taste of a peach or an apricot is not to be regarded as anything mysterious or impossible to communicate. It is simply to be given a scientific description in terms of inputs such as tissue damage, outputs such as avoidance behaviour, and whatever further information neurophysiology can give us. It is clearly possible to think that all this can be replicated by computer technology, and to conclude that computers, or sophisticated robots, could feel pain. That is the argument of the physicalist.

The Importance of Feelings

Arguments against saying that humans are mere machines have to appeal to subjective experience and its felt characteristics. They have to rely on what is apparently beyond the remit of science. Traditional empiricist philosophy has relied heavily on the notion of subjective experience. The world, it thought, is precisely what can be experienced. The bedrock of knowledge has been seen as 'impressions' or 'sense-data'. The very idea of empiricism is bound up with that of subjective experience. Science, for many philosophers, is built on this. The inherent subjectivity and private nature of such experience has generally been mitigated by the argument that it can be shared in normal circumstances so that it is 'intersubjective'. Nevertheless, it is ironic that a philosophy which has historically been the bedrock of science finds itself challenged by some modern versions of naturalist philosophy. Whatever the limitations of empiricism, it provided a rationale for the building of scientific knowledge.

Are the sensed characteristics of subjective experience to be dismissed so easily? Are they just physical processes, with no intrinsic felt character? Whatever their connection with such processes, it seems difficult and contrary to common sense and 'folk psychology', to deny the central importance in human life of looks, tastes, sounds and sensations. There is surely something it is like to experience such things. This has little to do with more general considerations about the role of reason, or the nature of the self. It is just a question whether mental content, of the simplest and most direct kind, is dispensable, by being viewed wholly in physical terms. Are my feelings, as viewed from the inside, identical with various events in particular parts of the brain, as detected by an actual or potential scanner? The same question can be asked about animals. What is it like to be a dog, for example, reliant on scent more than sight? Can this be replicated scientifically? Even if a canine robot were built which behaved exactly like a real dog, and could discriminate between smells, would it be able to smell? Would it have the experiences of an ordinary dog? Reacting to a particular stimulus may not be all that is involved in having an experience.

Arguments have raged about this in philosophy, and indeed the nature of consciousness is one of the most controversial subjects of all. Is seeing colour the same as being able to discriminate between colours? What of people who saw colours in a systematically different way, with, say, the spectrum inverted? What would we say of somebody who could identify red objects, but in fact sees red in the way that we would normally see green? The situation is complicated by the fact that this may not be detectable, but is clearly conceivable. We may well think that seeing red is something that cannot be captured in anything other than the experience. Pain is another favourite example, not least because of its undoubted importance in human life.[6] Just as some people are colour-blind and do not see certain colours properly, it is possible to be congenitally insensitive to pain. Some people just do not feel pain, even though they are not numb and can feel warmth and other such sensations. Such a condition is not just an interesting curiosity. It is highly dangerous, as an important warning signal of tissue damage is absent. People can sit on hot radiators and not realize they have been burnt. They can run barefoot on sharp pebbles on a beach and not realize that their feet have been lacerated.

This is not a case of indifference to pain, of feeling it and not minding it. Something is just lacking. No doubt a physical cause can in principle be found. Whatever problems there may be in normal neurological functioning, it is the absence of the distinctive feeling we call 'pain' that is the main feature of this condition. One patient thought that she was learning to feel pain, and became more adept at picking up cues to possible injury, thus avoiding dangerous situations. Avoidance of injury, however, is not the same as feeling pain. Doctors concluded that that particular patient still could feel no pain. Reactions to pain, such as distress and finding it unpleasant, together with physical reactions, such as avoidance, may be normal accompaniments of pain. Perhaps they enable us to teach and learn the words through public manifestations, but they are not part of the intrinsic nature of the experience. Yet many philosophers, and not just those with materialist leanings, find this idea of a sensation having an intrinsic quality hard to accept.

Wittgenstein famously opposed the idea of any private language about our own sensations. He did not think that we could refer to them, or even think of them, in terms which were not accessible to other people. He held that any identification and re-identification of our private feelings had somehow to be anchored in the public world. For him, a public language was in effect prior to any private thought or experience. He was not willing to accept the idea that we made private judgements which could not be checked publicly. This champions the irrelevance of the private stage, if perhaps not its unreality. There would, he fears, in the case of introspection, be no difference between thinking we were right about our feelings, even when we were not, and actually being right. This view was as much aimed against the empiricist idea of 'sense-data' (thought of as the basis of our knowledge of the world) as against identifications of pain. Nevertheless, there is a presupposition that thought and experience must be logically dependent on a shared, public language. According to this, we cannot think or have experiences unless we can speak. A language is obviously very important in helping us to form our thoughts and to express them. It is not, though, obvious that we cannot be conscious of something, or have private thoughts, unless we can speak. What of infants or animals? Might a small child or an animal not feel pain, just because it has no words to describe it? Making the learning of language more important than the immediate experience of our private feelings will have that consequence.

We often think that our sensations have particular qualities, which are sometimes difficult to put into words. The word 'pain' covers a range of sensations which still seem to have something in common and can be distinguished from other kinds of unpleasant sensations. Even in ordinary language we appear to distinguish between pains and unpleasant sensations, such as those from electric shocks or nausea. This seems to be related to the intrinsic characteristics of the sensation. Wittgenstein, however, would find it difficult to distinguish between a pain and our expression of it in behaviour. He makes the latter the criterion of the former, and the means by which we learn what a pain is. Nevertheless, the idea of pain as a distinctive kind of sensation, which may normally trigger a certain kind of response, seems hard to eradicate. Pain is a warning signal and we are normally programmed to react to it in particular ways. Yet there is such a thing as the quality of a sensation. Pain is the obvious example, but all of our sensations, located in the body, have a special 'feel' of various kinds. We know how they feel, whatever may be actually going on in our body.

We can often correlate each feeling with some physical episode. No one suggests that the mind and body merely operate in parallel and are not intimately involved with each other. The philosophical question remains, however, of the exact relation between the two. There is an argument that arises from scientific theory itself which suggests that a tough physicalist analysis is deficient. Since feelings and sensations seem so important to humans, and no doubt to many animals as well, a question must surely be posed of their evolutionary purpose. They cannot be merely dismissed as illusory or unimportant in the way that some materialists seem to do. Why do we feel pain at all, if the same result could have been obtained by physical machinery through reflex mechanisms and the like? Being told that we do not feel pain at all would seem ludicrous. We are not usually numb, otherwise there would be no need for anaesthetics. Being told that pain is really a neural event may appear scientific, but this does not tell us why we should feel anything in the first place. The neural event itself could be sufficient to cause avoidance action without us feeling anything. That might have been a kinder solution, given the agony that many suffer. The suspicion must remain that a feeling like pain is itself a product of evolution. The case of congenital insensitivity to pain illustrates the point. A warning of tissue damage is beneficial. Being deprived of it is dangerous.

The question still remains as to why the warning should take conscious form. Perhaps a conscious memory can be an important guide to future action, just as awareness of present pain can give us an opportunity to do something about it. Automatic reactions may be appropriate sometimes, as when we snatch our hands away from something hot, without stopping to think. Even this is often a response to pain rather than a simple reflex action. Often, however, an ability to decide the right response gives us the freedom of choice and an ability to adapt to a situation. This adds up to a prized flexibility which can be evolutionarily advantageous. Whatever the answer, the fact of pain gives humans an advantage that mere physiological machinery cannot. Even in the case of animals, the fear of future pain, given the memory of previous pain, can form a useful guide to behaviour.

The development of mind should not be mysterious from an evolutionary point of view. Yet, as the physicalist will point out, this suggests that mind is somehow based on the transmission of physical characteristics, under genetic control. No evolutionary theory could account for some mysterious addition of any new substance. If, then, minds, or at least mental properties, are to be taken seriously, they have to be related to material processes. This viewpoint is reinforced by seeing a continuum between animals and humans, particularly in the case of mental properties such as pain.

Many philosophers try to relate the mental closely to its physical grounding, while still taking its apparent reality seriously. They have no wish to join the ranks of the eliminative materialists, but are attracted to a broadly physicalist programme. Their problem is how to acknowledge the reality of the mental, while not accepting what they see as the metaphysical mystery of dualism. They are monists, believing in one substance not two, and accepting the ultimate reality of the physical alone. They think that they can do this by insisting on the dependence of 'higher order' mental states on 'lower order' physical ones. The former are said to 'supervene' on the latter. 'Supervenience' is a tricky notion, and its purpose is to avoid the absurdity of eliminative materialism, while stressing the priority of the physical. The crunch question, however, must be whether mental states are themselves understood as having any causal powers on their own. Common sense would suggest that they do. Apart from the effect of pain on our bodies, conscious desires would often seem to have a significant effect on behaviour. Beliefs, true or not, can be powerful driving forces. The very idea of the 'psychosomatic' suggests that our understanding can affect the whole state of bodies. A materialist, however, who is happy to talk of beliefs and desires, would still think of them as supervenient on physical states. In other words, it is the underlying state that provides the motive force, not the mental contents. If the mental states are not merely discounted, it is very difficult to avoid seeing them then as mere 'epiphenomena', appearances that are not part of the ordinary causal story of my life. They are like the froth on top of a fast-flowing river, caused by the real currents flowing underneath, but having no possibility of having any effect itself on the river.

Emergence and Causation

Another way of describing the situation is by talking of so-called 'emergence'. The idea of an emergent property calls attention to the fact that physical systems gain new properties as they grow in complexity. The whole is often more than the sum of its parts. This is a deliberate rebuttal of the urge to reduce everything to talk of the behaviour of components, whether they are sub-atomic particles, genes or some other chosen unit. The very fact that genes are thought of as having their own properties suggests that the analysis of everything at the level of micro-physics would leave important features out of account. Biology itself would have no content as a science, if physics was adequate to explain everything.

The idea of emergent properties is superficially attractive, but the notion of emergence is itself far from clear. Perhaps what is meant is that there are different levels, perhaps like the levels of tall office blocks, where one depends on the other, and without it could not continue to exist. The seventh floor would have known nothing to rest on if there was not a sixth floor. The problem with this image is that each level has an identity of its own, and no doubt there can be traffic and messages from the seventh to the sixth floor, as well as in the opposite direction. To take the analogy back to the mind and the brain, it may seem as if the mind depends on the architecture of the brain, and does not float in the middle of the sky apart from it. Yet it must have its own identity, and can influence the body, just as the body influences the mind. This, though, is to grant more autonomy to the mind than materialists wish. For them, the mind is not just produced by the brain, and is now independent of it. They want to put forward a 'non-reductive materialism' that allows talk of the mind, while refusing to give it any causal powers of its own.

One example of someone who wants to talk of emergence, while still claiming to be a physicalist, is the American philosopher John Searle. He gives examples of 'causally emergent' features of systems, such as the physical properties of solidity, liquidity and transparency. Solidity, for instance, is definitely a property of the table, but not of the physical particles that comprise it. It is a property of the system and not of its elements. The same applies to the liquidity of water, as well as its other properties. Water can put out fires, but oxygen, one of its components, will make them burn more fiercely. Searle regards consciousness as a similar kind of emergent property, holding of a system, but not of its components. That means that matter itself could not be conscious on its own, unless it is organized in a particular way in a brain. It then produces consciousness in the same way that hydrogen and oxygen in combination produce liquidity. Searle writes: 'The existence of consciousness can be explained by the causal interactions between elements of the brain at the micro level, but consciousness itself cannot be deduced or calculated from the sheer physical structure of the neurons without some additional account of the causal relations between them.'[7] In other words, consciousness can be explained causally, as the outcome of relations between neurons, when organized in a system. The account is a thoroughly physicalist one, making consciousness the product of a physical system. It cannot be ultimately explained in its own terms, but has to be transformed into physical ones. What goes on in the upper storey is not independent of the lower one, it appears, but is determined by what happens downstairs.

Searle himself makes this abundantly clear when he distinguishes his view of 'emergence' from one which suggests that consciousness is somehow 'squirted out', so as to have a life of its own. That would be a form of dualism. He regards consciousness as much more intimately related to physical structure. One cannot have solidity without a solid object, and one cannot be conscious without having the requisite neuronal architecture. This treads a fine line between physicalism and dualism. Either consciousness is just a matter of neuronal structure, or it emerges to be something independent. If it emerges and yet is not independent, it is hard to see that the materialism inherent in the position is very different from the reductive materialism it is challenging. The main contrast being made appears to be a conceptual one. We can, it seems, use our mental concepts and our normal language for talking of the mind, without being told it is all folk psychology.

Much depends on the idea of the emergence. Liquidity is more a description of a physical system than an attribution of new causal powers. For many, however, the whole point of talking about emergent properties is that the new properties are not just new ways of describing a complicated system of physical components, in relation with each other. Many theories are prepared to talk of new properties which actually have an influence on the components. Systems are 'self-organizing', and the whole becomes more than its parts, so that the parts behave in the system in ways they would not in isolation. More comes out of less. All this is controversial. Does an avalanche become more than its physical components? Is a tornado a force in its own right, so that the physical system constrains the random movements of its individual parts? Similarly, we talk of traffic jams, and traffic engineers may find it convenient to assume that they have a momentum of their own. It might well be, however, that they are the result of the individual decisions of hundreds of motorists, producing consequences, none of which are intended. The whole would then be still explicable in terms of its parts.

As with so many philosophical disputes, this was foreshadowed by Plato. One of his examples was a sentence which appears to be more than the list of words making it up. Yet whether a physical system is or is not more than the sum of its components, the point is that it is still physical. This is the issue in the case of mind. Materialists look for causal explanations in terms of upwards causation. Everything about the building is explained in terms of what goes on in the basement. Others are not so sure. What is decided on in the directors' suite on the top floor may surely influence activities in the lower storeys. The mind can influence the body, not just because it is itself part of the body. Mental events are distinct, some will maintain. They are not just elegant ways of talking of neuronal events. They describe a fresh level.

Any view that does not properly accept the distinctive character of the mental level is not treating it as something that can genuinely have an influence. 'Top-down' causation in the case of the mind is not just a summary of complicated neuronal interactions. It must imply that the behaviour of neurons is different from what it would otherwise be because of the influence of the new property. In this way, any meaningful idea of 'top-down' causation must regard mental properties as distinct. This might involve a property dualism, since it is hard to see how properties, such as pain, could be regarded as causally effective if the only causes can be physical. The idea of emergence is exceedingly slippery in a materialist framework. A dualist can quite happily accept the acquisition of new types of properties, causally produced by the brain, but perhaps themselves able to have physical effects. For the materialist or physicalist, however, mental properties are constituted in a strong sense by the processes of the brain. They cannot be effects, with a certain measure of independence.

The question remains how mental properties could have causal powers. Pain could not achieve anything in a materialist framework which a combination of neurons could not. Feelings become irrelevant in the functioning of the real world. It seems that emergent properties, or new levels, depend totally for what they are on a physical substratum, and that the direction of causation can only go from the bottom up. Properties could scarcely influence or change the very physical conditions which constitute them. They are composed of neurons and cannot affect them, since they would be affecting themselves. Every effect they produce can and will be achieved by the neurons themselves. The idea of downward causation becomes an illusion without an element of what must be turned 'dualism' in the system. Solidity cannot change the character of my desk, but is merely a description of its physical character.

Pain, however, let alone more complicated mental characteristics like decisions, purposes and intentions, can, it is often thought, alter physical states. My beliefs can even control the pain I feel. A player, for example, could be so absorbed in attempting to score a try in a rugby match that he does not feel the pain of a broken limb until he has completed his run. The mind, it seems, can concentrate on one thing to the exclusion of others. Sometimes it is possible to do this deliberately. What I choose to do, or think about, controls my bodily responses. This, though, brings us back to the question of rationality and choice, which raise even larger questions than 'simple' questions of dualism between mind and body. The role of reason has always taken centre stage, and it is this to which we must return.

Notes

1   Paul M. Churchland, *The Engine of Reason, the Seat of the Soul*, MIT Press, Cambridge, MA,1995, p. 18.
2   E. O. Wilson, *Consilience*, Alfred A. Knopf, New York, 1998, p. 96.
3   Ray Kurzweil, *The Age of Spiritual Machines*, Penguin Books, New York, 1999, p. 6.
4   Daniel Dennett, *Consciousness Explained*, Little, Brown, Boston, MA, 1991, p. 16.
5   Churchland, *The Engine of Reason*, p. 23.
6   See my *Pain and Emotion*, Oxford University Press, Oxford, 1970, for a defence of the idea of an intrinsic quality for pain.
7   John Searle, *The Rediscovery of the Mind*, MIT Press, Cambridge, MA, 1992, p. 112.

10

Reason and Philosophy

Reason and Matter

Consciousness is a mystery in many people's eyes. Once it has been explained in physical terms, its most important features seem to have been left out of account. It has been explained away, but hardly explained. This is perhaps inevitable, since the aim of the physicalist programme is to explain consciousness in terms that do not invoke consciousness. This simply changes the subject. The position is all the more poignant when it is realized that scientists and philosophers, in attempting to explain consciousness, are doing so through the medium of their own consciousness.

Consciousness is a matter of more than just tastes and smells, sensations and colours, important though these may be. Self-consciousness becomes of vital importance at the human level. We are conscious of our own mental processes, as well as the world outside us. There is a reflexivity about reasoning and understanding that enables us to reflect on our own rationality. Talk of 'feedback mechanisms' hardly does justice to this experience. We are aware of ourselves as selves, as subjects making choices and decisions, and being responsible for them. That does not mean that I can somehow stumble upon myself. Hume once famously argued against this. He pointed out that he could never discover the self apart from particular perceptions. I am always hot or cold, loving or hating, and so on. I am never just me. Hume concluded that selves were just bundles of perceptions. There was no ultimate, metaphysical substance. Yet this means that there is not even a principle of unity, linking the perceptions in a bundle. They have no owner.

Attacks on the self have become more prevalent in modern philosophy.

They come from various directions, from postmodernism as much as physicalism. The idea of a self is very metaphysical and cannot easily be reduced to the brain. For many, it is too reminiscent of religious doctrines of the soul, of what purports to make a person the individual he or she is. They may prefer to use the body as a criterion of personal identity. That, indeed, is the way we normally pick each other out, but there is a further question as to whether that is all we actually are. Postmodernists certainly rule out all metaphysics and typically regard selves as constructions. Who we are depends on how our culture regards us and how we regard ourselves, rather than being some form of pure 'essence'. Selves then become little different from narrative stories, binding disparate events together in apparent patterns. We are the people we imagine ourselves to be.

Metaphysics is in this way discarded and everything becomes the result of novel writing without an author. Despite the desire of postmodernism to see science like this, Dennett, a devotee of science, is happy to view the self in a thoroughly postmodernist way. He sees it as the product of ' the story we tell others - and ourselves - about who we are'.[1] Our tales, he says, are not spun. They spin us, so that we are the product, not their source. He believes that there are in the brain what he terms 'multiple drafts', according to which 'all varieties of thought or mental activity are accomplished in the brain by parallel, multi-track processes of interpretation and elaboration of sensory inputs'.[2] This line of thought inevitably dissolves the unity of the mind into different physical processes. Dennett quite explicitly accepts that there is nowhere where everything comes together, no central director pulling the different themes into a harmonious whole. As another materialist, E. O. Wilson, says: 'There is no single stream of consciousness, in which all information is brought together by an executive ego'.[3] The brain may actually work with streams of parallel processing. That is a matter for neurophysiology. Whether that is all that can be said about the mind depends on the prior view of whether science is the only source of knowledge. Does it follow from the fact that science cannot discover a 'central controller' that there is none? The problem is that scientific judgement itself calls for a rational comparison of different data. This involves the exercise of independent judgement, bringing together the significance of a variety of events and experiences. Science itself needs a conception of a rational subject, which can relate different evidence acquired at different times.

Any materialist, and determinist, position undercuts our claims to be rational if rationality is thought distinct from forms of causation. Even in the archetypal case of billiard balls, explanation for their movement will always be the way the cue is held and the way they are struck by it and strike each other. It is never in terms of the reason for which they are struck, or the way in which a player may be aiming at a particular pocket. Yet without the context of the game and the purposes of each player, the movement of the balls will seem more random than they actually are. A materialist explanation can no more be concerned with truth as a goal, than causal accounts can take any notice of the pockets of a billiard table. Rationality, however, is forward looking and concerned with truth, at least when it is a question of which beliefs are to be adopted and assertions uttered. This discussion is haunted by the fear that metaphysical entities should not be allowed into our scheme of things. We should not think that anything exists unless it is located in the world of space and time, subject to physical laws. We have already seen how the idea of such a law is far from clear cut. So is the notion of physics, which can mean anything from views that happen to be held by contemporary physicists, to what one day could in principle be held by some rational being somewhere. The idea that a monist position, relying on 'physical' states alone, removes all philosophical problems is very naive.

We all know how to reason and to question what is true. The very issue of the status of dualism, and that of physicalism, only arises because of our possession of rationality. That cannot simply be ignored or eliminated because of the assumptions of materialism. We may still wonder about the connection between reason and the workings of the physical world. Saying, however, that this is a scientific question is already to take up a philosophical position about the primary role of the physical world and of our ability to understand it. Yet that is to assume that philosophy itself is possible and indeed necessary. We are back with the question as to what makes us able to reason philosophically, and whether the content of our reasoning can be adequately translated into terms accessible to science.

Can We Accept the Non-material?

A consistent theme in philosophy from its origins in the ancient Greek world has been the distinction between appearance and reality. Science itself shows that physical reality is not what it seems. Philosophy, however, goes much further, and deals with the reality underlying all the scientific information we amass. It does not just deal with what does exist, but with what can exist. It deals with the conditions of possibility of an activity like science, and, at its best, also deals with the nature of reality. Those who wish to deny that anything could exist outside the physical world have to dismiss appearances as merely that, and perhaps not even that. Our mental processes are not accepted as part of the real world. Not only, it seems, are they illusory, but some would hold that they are not even real illusions. They have no existence at all, and our language is mistaken even in referring to them. The reality is only the physical state. This certainly makes the assimilation of human to machine intelligence much easier.

Can anyone, however, actually rule out the existence of the non-material? It is always difficult to prove a negative, or to drop restrictions on the development of science. Many put their faith in science as the sole source of knowledge precisely because they want to rule out spiritual or ghostly entities. Ghosts are in fact a good example. There are often reports of strange phenomena involving, say, alleged poltergeists flinging objects around. The effects of these supposed activities are certainly open to empirical investigation. Similarly, apparitions are seen, or claimed to be seen, in old houses. Mysterious presences are 'felt'. So one could go on. Is any of this significant? Those following in the empiricist tradition of Hume would be inclined to argue that we do not normally experience such things. The conclusion seems to be that we cannot, or at least should not, take reports of them on trust. Why should we believe them? If they go against all our customary experience of the world it may seem more likely that the reports are mistaken or misleading, rather than that they are true, and upset all our understanding of how the world works. Similar reasoning perhaps may lead many to be sceptical of unidentified flying objects. They are more likely to be either hallucinations, it may be said, or the mistaken interpretation of ordinary phenomena - perhaps a new kind of aircraft has been identified as something alien.

Reports of paranormal events need not be taken at face value, even if we accept them. I was once told of how whoever slept in a particular room in an old house tended to have the same dream of being pushed over a cliff. Not surprisingly, the room got something of a reputation, until it was discovered that the house was built on sinking foundations on made-up ground in a ditch just outside an ancient city wall. The room and bed were at an angle, and there was a natural explanation for what might seem an almost supernatural occurrence. This is a simple example and a warning against undue credulity. Not all odd experiences must have a supernatural explanation. Perhaps none do.

In the end, however, the decision as to whether reports of abnormal phenomena should be dismissed becomes a philosophical one. The question is whether we should dismiss even a trustworthy and reliable witness who reports something which goes against customary experience. It does not follow that science could never account for such experiences, even if it cannot do so at the moment. Some believe that even so-called 'supernatural' phenomena, connected with ghostly apparitions, might be explicable in scientific terms one day. There is a real sense in which limiting our vision to the horizon of current science also blocks the possibility of future science. Some naturalists could of course accept that, although the notion of an ideal science begins to get somewhat metaphysical. The crunch question comes when we wonder whether some realities might be beyond the reach even of possible human science. Might there be another domain besides the physical one? We are back with questions about a Platonic dualism. Even if the other world was not a world of Forms, of ideal standards, but had some other character, could we ever have any reason for conceiving of its existence? Would such a metaphysical realm be in the same position as other physical universes, with which we could have no contact? The point, though, would not be that such a world need be beyond our reach. It would just be of a different kind from any physical realm, perhaps outside any spatio-temporal framework. This would be more radical than separating mind and body. Whatever their relation to physical occurrences, mental events are still part of our current spatio-temporal world. Pains are located in the body and have a duration, even if they are not themselves physical objects.

Talking of the possibility of a different non-physical realm is not necessarily the same as postulating some spiritual domain. In Western thought, references to God do pose just this kind of question. As we have already seen, however, a realm of numbers would also be a candidate for a non- physical world outside space and time. The issue is not just whether such worlds could exist, but whether arguments about them are a legitimate and important part of philosophy. Separating reality from human knowledge of it might make it perfectly proper to talk of the possibility of realms independent of human understanding. They cannot be totally separate from humans, however, or we would be oblivious of them. Any philosophical doctrine of different 'levels' of reality would have to show how one level could be accessible from another. Plato's world of Forms is a case in point. He could not have postulated ideal standards if we could have had no inkling of their existence. How could we even know enough to say that there were any, let alone what they were? The temptation when faced with such metaphysical claims is always to wield Ockham's razor and not multiply entities, let alone worlds. Against this, however, should be put Einstein's saying that everything should be made as simple as possible, but not simpler.

Faced with a complex reality, simplicity is not a virtue. It should be a guide to truth, not a substitute for it. If there really were Platonic Forms, ruling them out by definition would be unhelpful. Plato was aware that he had to give an account of how we could have a conception of them. He claimed that we were born with innate ideas of them, which we were able to learn how to recollect. He was thus able to give an explanation as to how a bridge existed between two realms. Needless to say, empiricist philosophers have always found this conception of innate ideas highly distasteful. Yet in philosophical terms it should not be the positing of non-material realms which is itself problematic. Why should we be in a position to put arbitrary limits on the nature of reality, any more than we should determine in advance the kind of things that we could experience? The real problem is how we can think or talk about something of which we appear to have no knowledge. We cannot, and it follows that we must have at least partial knowledge to have any conception of something at all. Any reference to a non-physical reality has to allow for some explanation as to how we could be in touch with it.

Two Worlds

When mysterious phenomena apparently occur within the physical world, this may give us a reason for thinking of something beyond it. Apart from Hume's epistemological objections, there is also the more basic metaphysical issue of what can and cannot exist. An empiricist will refuse to accept the need for going beyond experience. If someone apparently experiences something mysterious, it will be considered a matter of having a strange experience rather than an experience of something strange. As Thomas Hobbes suggested from the standpoint of his seventeenth-century materialism, those who say that God speaks to them in dreams are perhaps merely saying that they dream that God speaks to them. The question is what warrants the extra step from experience to reality.

A similar issue arises in the case of so-called near-death experiences. Many people at the point of death do have extraordinary experiences, ranging from a review of their past life, and out-of-the-body experiences, to apparent experiences of a life to come. Sometimes they have a 'vision' of relatives who have already died. An extra twist in the latter case is that there are reports of visions of close relatives who had died shortly before, without the knowledge of the person having the experience. These experiences are not culturally specific. Plato himself reports one in the so-called 'myth of Er' in the tenth book of the *Republic*. A soldier, Er, is rescued from a funeral pyre. After having apparently died, he revives and then tells of his experiences beyond death.

It is perhaps not too fanciful to draw a parallel between this vision, giving a mystical experience of a realm beyond our present one, and Plato's own philosophical views. He believes that the philosophers should escape from the ordinary sights and sounds of the shadowy world around us and obtain knowledge in the pure light of truth. This conception of the purpose of philosophy in this life is perhaps similar to the ideas apparently underlying near-death experiences. There is the same distinction between two worlds, and a passage from one to the other. In the allegory of the cave in the *Republic*, Plato describes how the soul has to escape the world of shadows and copies, and get out to the realm of pure sunlight where it could see things for what they really are. There is a contrast between the uncertain and partial knowledge we have now, and the knowledge of the truth which can be obtained in another realm of pure light, illuminating everything. This has been a fairly constant theme in Western philosophy and religion. The link between knowledge and light, or illumination, is very deeply embedded in our thought. Paradoxically it is one that was much used in the Enlightenment, at the same time that the idea of two worlds was being attacked. It is, however, not a conception that could easily be stated within a modern scientific world-view. It is too mystical and perhaps too subjective, since it is not easily amenable to public testing. Postmodernism would perhaps find it more difficult to rule out, in that the imagery constitutes an ongoing tradition of thought. Yet since its whole point is to stress the existence, and perhaps the accessibility, of some absolute standard of truth and meaning, it is bound to be at loggerheads with any attempt to undermine the objectivity of truth. The Enlightenment may have brought a mystical conception of truth down to earth, but it did still maintain a vision of truth as a goal.

The fear of the Platonic panoply of two worlds still drives much modern materialism. The latter thrives on the threat of the former. The stark choice is sometimes presented between the rigour of scientific method and the credulity of a philosophy that apparently makes large claims with little basis. The philosophical pendulum has often moved from those who said that mind is the only reality to those who claimed that matter was, and then back again. The deficiencies and exaggerations of one view only encourage a reaction to the other. Both are philosophical positions which can call on serious arguments in their defence, but they are not the only alternatives.

There are intermediate positions which can take both matter and mind seriously, in a way that can give proper scope to science, without assuming that it has all the answers.

The confrontation between materialism and its opponents does illustrate that arguments about what can exist are central to philosophy. Materialists may sometimes pretend that they are simply following the discoveries of science, but the idea that they have to is, as we have constantly maintained, philosophical. Philosophy is not just a matter of logic or clarification of the use of language. These are some of its tools but, at root, philosophy must be concerned with our relation to the world. It must deal with what there is, ontology, and how far it can be known, epistemology. Subservience to science can only restrict these aims. We look at what humans actually happen to know as opposed to what they ought to. The inevitable result is to remove our confidence that scientific 'knowledge' is worthy of that name. The fact that many want to challenge the status of science shows how a philosophical defence of science is essential.

Philosophy deals with the most profound questions facing us as human beings. The kind of world we live in, and our relation to it, not only affects how we live. Our own understanding of it also has a major influence on the way we conduct our lives. It is an argument against materialism that an apparently abstract belief in materialism itself can be a salient factor in people's lives, simply because it is a belief. It governs what they think important. A philosophical outlook, in other words, can make a real difference in the world.

The restriction of the idea of reason to science and its methods itself fuelled the rejection of any kind of rationality. Modernity has bred postmodernity. Those sceptical of the role of science in human life have identified scientific rationality with rationality as such. The self, as the subject of rationality, has also been a casualty, as has been the reality about which we can reason. Richard Rorty is quite happy to demolish the distinctions which he sees built into the vocabulary we inherited from Plato and Aristotle. He says (speaking as an 'anti-Platonist' accused of relativism): 'Our opponents like to suggest that to abandon their vocabulary is to abandon rationality - that to be rational consists precisely in respecting the distinctions between the absolute and the relative, the found and the made, object and subject, nature and convention, reality and appearance.'[4] His (philosophical) argument is that these distinctions are not essential to philosophy, any more presumably than are such binary opponents as the self and the other, or even truth and falsity. The danger in all this is that of losing grip altogether on the idea of rationality, the idea that there are norms for belief, so that we ought to believe some things and reject others. It is all too easy to settle for what people do believe, and, if they disagree, to resort to a relativism that suggests that differences in belief do not matter. Indeed, 'pluralism' becomes something to be welcomed. Philosophy ceases to be a matter of rational criticism. It is hard to see how it can then have any function at all. It must become absorbed into the general cultural stream. Philosophers can then articulate the assumptions of one cultural tradition in a way that is irrelevant to the members of another.

Rorty explicitly allies himself with American pragmatism, an important philosophical tradition, but one which has clearly come from a specific cultural background. Genuine philosophy must aspire to universality. American pragmatism must stand on its merits, and not on the fact that it is American. Relativism cannot allow this, and there is nowhere for Rorty to stand to allow him to recommend his views to those beyond his own tradition. It is not enough to be an American speaking to Americans or, in an even more restricted way, an American East Coast liberal speaking to American East Coast liberals. Philosophical justification has to demonstrate why the views of such people are relevant to those with different backgrounds. By attacking traditional conceptions of rationality, Rorty can narrow the scope and impact of philosophy, so that any distinction from the rest of culture is removed. Just as an unremitting, literally mindless, materialism can dissolve reason into a series of physical events, so relativism dissolves philosophy into a series of cultural stances. The one makes philosophy cede its position to science, and the other to sociology or cultural studies. Philosophy becomes impotent, without any distinction between what seems to us to be so and what is so, or might be. What is the point of criticisms or questions if we cannot be wrong? There is no point in examining the basis of our beliefs if the most important fact is merely that we have them, and not whether they are true.

Philosophy Matters

Philosophy matters if we think reason matters. It becomes important when we realize that what we think is not a mere matter of physiological causation or social convention. It is paradoxical that the very philosophical arguments which champion doctrines such as materialism or relativism, suggest that philosophy is irrelevant. Yet if it is irrelevant, and reason is an illusion, such doctrines could not be promulgated in the first place.

How then can reason be justified? How can a trust in rationality be shown to be more than a passing phase of European history? There is obviously something very peculiar about giving reasons in favour of reason. Does that mean it cannot be justified? This way of putting the problem is misguided. If humans possess rationality, its use is not an option. It is as fundamental to human life as the fact that we normally possess senses to enable us to track events in the outside world. In the last resort, it is impossible to justify perception without appealing to all other instances of perception. We have to take it on trust that most people normally do see the world correctly. My perceptions can be checked by yours. Perception as such cannot be. Philosophical scepticism may be a challenging intellectual exercise, but it is a hopeless way to live a life, as Hume himself recognized. We can question the scope of human reason and we use our reason to question and criticize. It still seems impossible to stand outside ourselves and to question (rationally) the fact of our own rationality. Descartes wanted to make God the guarantor of our ability to reason properly, but then tried rationally to establish the existence of God. He was caught in a hopeless circle. No doubt, if there is a God, the fact that we can reason is grounded in some way in His will for us. We cannot, though, argue rationally for the existence of God with the express purpose of providing a firm ground for the possibility of rational argument. We cannot assume what we want to demonstrate. Rationality is an indispensable precursor of everything we think, say and do. We cannot think philosophically without it, and questioning its existence from a philosophical viewpoint merely begs the question. Using success in science as a justification is no more convincing. We cannot decide what is a success without using the very reason that we are trying to uphold.

Does this mean that we have to assume the efficacy of reason before we start reasoning? One line of argument, following an approach favoured by Kant, would make certain beliefs or stances a precondition of whatever activity we undertake. The activity would depend on them. Nicholas Rescher provides a typical instance of this form of reasoning. He says that the foundations of objectivity do not rest on the findings of science. He continues: 'They precede and underlie science, which would not itself be possible without a commitment to the capacity of our senses to warrant claims about an objective world order. Objectivity is not a product of inquiry: we must commit ourselves to it to make inquiry possible.'[5] Objectivity, he holds, has to have as its ultimate justification a so-called 'transcendental argument'. That means that it is 'an essential part of the projects of communication and inquiry as we standardly conduct them'. In other words, we could not communicate with each other, and conduct the inquiry, let alone a scientific one, without making certain assumptions. The existence of the practices are themselves a justification. The practices exist and therefore the assumptions that make them possible are validated. Interestingly, this view has its roots in the same American pragmatism that leads Rorty to dispense with the whole idea of the objectivity of truth. For Rescher, all our communication and inquiry is made possible by crucial assumptions. He says: 'we communally inhabit a shared world of objectively existing things, a world of "real things" among which we live and into which we inquire'.[6] Yet, he adds, we have to assume that the information we have at any time is imperfect and incomplete.

All this is true. We cannot think or speak without an assumption that truth is at stake. We cannot do science without being committed to an understanding that we live in a shared, objective world. Does the fact of science, or the fact of language, prove that our assumptions are right? Our science works and we do talk to each other, so we might conclude that our reason is reliable. Yet this kind of transcendental argument, justifying assumptions on the basis of the existence of a practice, does not prove as much as one would hope. Pragmatists could hope for nothing more, since they regard the existence of a practice as justification enough.

As postmodernist critics of rationality suggest, however, the mere existence of science is insufficient. Why should anyone continue to participate in it? If its conduct presupposes rationality and objectivity, an attack on the latter concepts may merely serve to show that science is impossible and its success wholly illusory. Anyone who believed that could not in all consistency be a scientist. One cannot participate in a practice while repudiating its foundations. One can, however, abstain from a practice. Much the same can be said about language. Perhaps the concepts of belief and assertion do imply distinctions between objective truth and falsity, a distinction between things being and not being the case. What is the point of saying anything, if one thing is as good as another? Yet the existence of language does not prove the sceptics wrong. The problem is that the assertion of scepticism uses linguistic categories that assume its opposite, not least the distinction between truth and falsity. The price of genuine scepticism may be silence. This may not help the philosophical defence of scepticism, but it does not prove it wrong, either. We may have to make certain assumptions to live our lives. It still makes sense to ask how far, and in what way, those assumptions are well-founded. We do not just need to understand the internal rationality of activities once they are undertaken. We need reasons for undertaking them, or not abstaining from them. It is not enough to use our reason. We hanker after some assurance that our trust in it is not misplaced. This becomes more pressing when rationality is derided as a passing historical phase, and philosophy is swept aside as having no serious function.

It is instructive that some philosophers think that reality is defined by scientific reason, whilst others think that they cannot refer to a real world with any confidence because rationality is culturally constructed. Both views implicitly link rationality with reality. The one tracks the other, it is thought, so that the concepts stand or fall together. Yet even this kind of explanation uses the very reason which we wish to justify. If our reason and the world are somehow in harmony with each other, must we just accept this as a basic fact? Certainly many philosophers would feel that they have no alternative. A pre-established harmony between human reasoning and the fundamental character of reality might seem an ambitious metaphysical thesis. Without it, however, it seems hard to trust what our reason tells us. Why, after all, should we assume that, at root, the world in its physical or metaphysical manifestations is intelligible to creatures like us at all? Reliance on the light of reason is all very well, but where does the light come from? When we look within science for an answer by appealing to natural selection, we are again assuming the truth of what we are trying to show. The harmony of human science with the world is being invoked to show that we are at home in the world.

Thomas Nagel, the contemporary American philosopher, deals with this issue, and points out that the conception of some natural sympathy 'between the deepest truths of nature, and the deepest layers of the human mind' makes many nervous.[7] There seems to be a fundamental connection between the human mind and an ordered world. Those who have talked of us being made in the image of God, or of reason being the candle of the Lord, may not have found this very surprising. We might then, in a limited way, think God's thoughts about the universe He had created. Nagel, on the other hand, thinks that the general nervousness about any harmony between mind and world is 'one manifestation of a fear of religion which has large and often pernicious consequences for modern intellectual life'.[8] Many, and Nagel admits that he is one, just want atheism to be true. Yet the function of reason, if it is to be possible at all, is to see things as they are, and not as we would like them to be. We must not be swayed by leanings to atheism or to religion. Philosophy itself can only be concerned with truth.

Any philosophy worthy of its name has to explore the fundamental relationship which we have with the world. Trouble arises when we adopt philosophical positions such as materialism or relativism that make the philosophical quest hopeless and pointless. We must never allow ourselves to undermine the possibility of the very intellectual activity we are engaged in, on the basis of its own findings. To do so would be to involve ourselves in the mire of contradiction.

Those who fashionably attack forms of dualism are also likely to attack the most fundamental distinction of all, the one between thinking and what we think about, our reason and the world. It is this which makes philosophy not just possible but necessary. Reality gives reason a target, and makes our own reflection on our activities within the world so vital. Without a self-conscious understanding of what we are about, we are liable to think and act uncritically, in ways that can be ultimately disastrous. If we do not know who we are, or where we are, how can we act with any autonomy or consistency, let alone wisdom? It is possible, as relativism does, to concentrate on our thoughts, without taking any notice of the fact that they are supposed to be about anything. Conversely, we can concentrate on the nature of the world, as materialism does, without taking any notice of the fact that we can reason about it. We can disclaim all responsibility. Holding the two, thought and reality, in tension with each other, serves to remind us that one function of philosophy should be to align the one with the other as far as possible. If we are truly to love wisdom (and the word 'philosophy' in Greek means the love of wisdom) we cannot afford to live in a world of illusion. That is one aspect of Plato's outlook which should command some support, whatever our modern illusions may be.

Philosophy is far too important a subject to be consigned to the periphery of our search for knowledge. It is not a superior form of mental gymnastics, playing around with logic or with words. It is not an upmarket form of the word-game 'Scrabble'. Without it, our understanding of our own intellectual life and of the world in which we are situated is at best narrowed, and at worst destroyed. Our own self-understanding, as rational beings set in a complicated universe, can guide our choices and direction. It can make us face up to our responsibilities and our limitations. It can help us to match our reasoning to the reality confronting us. None of this is possible without a rigorous examination even of the things we take most for granted.

The ancient Greeks believed that an unexamined life is not worth living. Perhaps in recent years philosophy has been too content to be packed off to the sidelines of intellectual life. It must not be afraid to regain its place at its heart, making us aware of our goals, the reasons for pursuing them, and giving us consistency in their pursuit. We should not rest content with a scientific search for the causes of people's beliefs. We cannot even merely acknowledge that they have them. We must not be afraid to exercise our own reason. There is no more important exercise of human rationality than philosophical reasoning. At its best, it can reach to the foundations of our thoughts and beliefs and expose them for what they are, solid or shaky, good or bad. Plato's ancient vision of philosophy saw it as the recovery of truth. The Enlightenment saw the acquisition of knowledge as synonymous with human progress and improvement. In a more cynical age, we should perhaps still acknowledge that there is a difference between truth and falsity. One can distinguish between rationality and irrationality. It does matter what we think. Philosophy is able to help us in that task. Philosophy matters too.

Notes

1   Daniel Dennett, *Consciousness Explained*, Little, Brown, Boston, MA, 1991, p. 418.
2   Ibid., p. 111.
3   E. O.Wilson, *Consilience*, Alfred A. Knopf, New York, 1998, p. 110.
4   Richard Rorty, *Philosophy and Social Hope*, Penguin Books, Harmondsworth, 1999, p. xix.
5   Nicholas Rescher, *A System of Pragmatic Idealism, Vol. 1, Human Knowledge in Idealistic Perspective*, Princeton University Press, Princeton, NJ, 1992, p. 258.
6   Ibid., p. 259.
7   Thomas Nagel, *The Last Word*, Oxford University Press, Oxford, 1997, p. 130.
8   Ibid.

Glossary

aesthetics   The theory of what constitutes good taste in artistic matters.

analytic philosophy   A modern tradition in philosophy which has stressed the importance of clarity and logical rigour in philosophical thinking. It has held that the main task of philosophy has been to analyse carefully the way we actually think.

anthropic principle   The contemporary scientific theory linking our existence with the initial conditions prevailing at the origin of the Universe. Any slight variation in those would have made human life impossible.

anthropocentric   Centred on, or dependent on, human beings.

anti-realism   The denial of the realist claim that reality is logically independent of human understanding.

appearance   What seems to be the case, in contrast to what may actually be so. The distinction between appearance and reality is a basic metaphysical one.

authority   The requirement that we give our obedience and respect to some person, institution or principle.

autonomy   The freedom to direct oneself without external constraint, perhaps in the form of authority or tradition.

belief   An attitude to the world distinguished from knowledge. Beliefs can be false, and may not be justified.

biology   The scientific study of living organisms and their development.

categorial framework   The system of concepts by which we structure and understand the world.

causal explanation   The account of how a state of affairs has been produced by an antecedent, and independent, state.

causation   The process whereby one event is produced by another independent one.

classical mechanics   The system of physics, deriving from Newton, to some extent superseded in the twentieth century by quantum mechanics.

common sense   The prevailing collective view of the world, often unexamined and taken for granted.

concept   The way we think of something and pick it out. Concepts can be shared, and are sometimes identified with the use of words in a language.

consciousness   A private awareness of the world, directly accessible to the subject, in a way that is not available to others.

constant conjunction   The consistent association of two distinct events. Hume considered this to be an adequate account of causation.

contingent   Whatever may or may not occur – contrasted with what is necessarily the case.

convention   Social acceptance through tacit or explicit agreement.

Copernican revolution   Kant's term for the structuring of reality by our concepts (instead of their reflecting reality). The analogy is with Copernicus's view that the earth goes round the sun and not vice versa.

deduction   The derivation of logically valid conclusions from a set of premisses. If the premisses are true, then so will be the conclusion.

deism   The belief in a God so separate from this world, that having created it he has no further contact with it. It was a particularly widespread view in the eighteenth century.

determinism   The view that every event has a cause. *Metaphysical* determinism is the claim that nothing in reality is uncaused. *Methodological* determinism is the decision to assume that everything is caused, and to look for causal explanations everywhere.

dualism   A belief in two distinct kinds of entity or category (such as the brain and the mind, or God and the world). *Property* dualism is the claim that there are two distinctive, and irreducible, types of property, normally the mental and physical. *Substance* dualism is the claim that there are two distinctive kinds of 'substances', or holders of properties, normally body and mind.

emergent property   Characteristics held by an entity or collection of entities, but not by the parts which constitute it. The whole is thus more than the sum of its parts.

empirical   Associated with human experience.

empiricism   The view that all knowledge is obtained from human experience.

Enlightenment, the   A movement extolling the central importance, and the autonomy, of human reason, in the place of authority and tradition. Widely seen as a phenomenon of the eighteenth century, its roots lie in the seventeenth.

epiphenomena   Referring to mental phenomena as distinct but powerless. They are the effects of physical states, but have themselves no causal efficacy.

epistemology   The philosophical study, and assessment, of the basis of our knowledge.

ethics   Reflection on the basis and justification of moral beliefs and behaviour.

evidence   Whatever indicates the truth or falsity of a claim.

evolution   The process by which different species acquire their characteristics through natural selection.

evolutionary epistemology   A philosophical theory about the basis of human knowledge, using Darwin's theory of evolution.

experience   A subjective awareness, often purporting to relate to something beyond itself, and normally the product of our senses.

folk psychology   Common-sense views about our minds, and their contents, derided by materialists as mistaken.

Forms   Sometimes called 'Ideas', these were regarded by Plato as objective, ideal and eternal standards, existing in a higher realm than the material world. They have various philosophical functions, including being 'universals' or common properties which their instances share.

free will   The ability to make uncaused, but rational and purposive, choices.

functionalism   A sophisticated contemporary philosophical theory about the nature of mind. It concentrates on the inputs and outputs of a physical system, such as the brain, or a computer, while ignoring the nature of any internal processing (such as 'consciousness').

genetic fallacy   The confusion of the origins of beliefs with issues concerning their validity and truth.

God's-eye view   The idea that it is possible to have a totally detached and disinterested outlook, transcending the limits of all particular perspectives. Other similar philosophical notions include a 'view from nowhere' and an 'absolute conception'.

idealism   The view that what exists depends on perception, or understanding, by minds.

ideology   A system of ideas normally seen as justifying the interests of their holders, but sometimes merely referring to any collective definition of reality.

incommensurability   The inability to compare, or translate, the terms of one theory with those of another.

induction   Generalizing our expectations, often in the form of physical laws, from now to another time, and from here to another place.

intentionality (of mind)   The way in which the contents of a mind can be directed at other, possibly non-existent, objects.

knowledge   True belief that is properly grounded in some manner.

laws of nature   Regularities and tendencies in the physical world. There have always been disputes as to how far such laws could be broken.

linguistic philosophy   A philosophical movement, flourishing in the middle of the twentieth century, which saw the precise analysis of our use of language as the main task of philosophy.

logical positivism   The movement initiated by the Vienna Circle in the 1920s and 1930s, which stressed the dual importance of experience and logical deduction in building up a scientific conception of the world.

materialism   The doctrine that only matter exists, and that everything, even the apparently mental, is composed of it. *Eliminative* materialism is an aggressive form of contemporary materialism concerning the nature of mind. It holds that all mental states are actually physical, and it wishes to remove the attributions of consciousness which so-called 'folk psychology' typically makes. *Non-reductive* materialism is the philosophical view that it is possible to uphold the sole reality of matter, whilst not eliminating emergent properties.

matter   Whatever constitutes the physical universe and is located in space and time. Modern physics finds it difficult to give the term a precise definition.

mechanism   Any system which operates only through the operation of cause and effect.

mechanistic   Operating through cause and effect, without purpose or intention.

metaphysics   The rational study of what lies beyond the scope of empirical investigation. As such, its very possibility has been contested by logical positivists, amongst others.

methodology   The theory of the aims and procedures of a discipline.

mind   A term covering at least whatever we are subjectively aware or conscious of, including thoughts and feelings, beliefs and desires.

modernity   The period (perhaps still with us) when immense faith was placed in the power of human reason in general and science in particular.

monism   The theory that only one type of thing (such as matter) constitutes reality.

mysticism   The search for experience of an ultimate divine reality.

natural selection   The biological process whereby different genetic types produce more or less offspring, and the fittest for their environment come to predominate over competitors.

naturalism   The view that reality is wholly accessible (at least in principle) to the natural sciences. Nothing (such as the 'supernatural') can exist beyond their reach. *Methodological* naturalism is the decision to look only for scientific explanations and to rule out any other kind.

necessary   What has to be the case, as opposed to what may or may not happen (and is thus contingent).

neo-Darwinism   The combination of Darwin's theory of evolution with modern genetic theory.

nihilism   The possibly incoherent view that nothing matters and that there is no such thing as truth. It is therefore a matter of indifference what one says, believes or does.

noumenal   Kant's term for what is only accessible through our understanding and not through our senses.

objectivity   The property of something being the case whatever human conceptions of it might be (also sometimes used merely to refer to detachment from all particular points of view, as in science).

Ockham's razor   The principle that one should not entertain the existence of logically superfluous entities. Named after William of Ockham, a medieval logician.

ontology   The philosophical theorizing about what there is.

opinion   A belief, which may, or may not, be true.

paradigm   An exemplar: a term used in the philosophy of science to signify starting points for traditions of scientific research.

phenomenal   What is accessible through the human senses.

philosophy   In Greek, the 'love of wisdom', the term has come to be applied to the examination of all our basic presuppositions. It relies on reasoning, as contrasted with empirical (or scientific) investigation.

physical   Whatever is accessible to physics, or reducible to it.

physicalism   The doctrine that everything can be explained in terms of physical laws (i.e. laws accepted by physics).

Physics   The scientific study of the basic constituents of the universe.

Platonism   Views depending on Plato's philosophy, particularly his dualist split between the world we are familiar with, and a higher realm of eternal Forms.

pluralism   The view that different theories and ways of life have to be accepted on equal terms, without one being judged superior.

postmodernism   A reaction against the Enlightenment conception of detached rationality. It stresses the way in which human judgements are made from within a particular perspective or tradition.

pragmatism   The philosophical view (originally American) that we always start from where we are with our present beliefs, and must reject metaphysics. All claims should be assessed in terms of the actual difference they make in the world.

private language   A language which can only be understood by one person. Its possibility was attacked by Wittgenstein, who stressed the social character of language.

progress   A process of cumulative improvement, so that change is directed and not arbitrary.

quantum mechanics   The modern physical theory, mathematically based, about the nature and behaviour of subatomic particles.

random   Contrasted with what happens for a purpose or reason.

rationalism   The belief in the power and scope of human reason. A narrower use of the term suggests that this entails atheism, but it is possible to hold that religious faith can be rationally based. Sometimes also used to refer to the philosophical tradition, opposed to empiricism, and typified by Descartes, which stresses the innate capabilities of reason, prior to experience.

rationality   An ability to reason in a detached manner to what one considers true conclusions.

rationalization   The giving of a rational explanation for action when it is not the real reason, or cause, of the action.

realism   The view that reality is logically independent of all conceptions, or descriptions, of it.

reduction   The demonstration that statements about one kind of entity are really about another (as in the case of the mind and the brain).

relativism   The view that there are different, possibly self-contained, traditions and ways of life, each to be judged only in accordance with its own standards. In particular, the view that 'truth' is a product of a particular social setting, and only has validity within that setting. *Conceptual* relativism is the view that the nature of our concepts depends on the particular society we belong to. The concepts of one society cannot be translated into those of another. *Cultural* relativism is the idea that the standards and beliefs of a culture (however defined) are not valid beyond its bounds. *Global* relativism is the position that all judgements, including scientific ones, can only claim truth within the context in which they were made. *Moral* relativism is the view that moral ideas, like rules of etiquette, only have relevance for the society holding them. They are matters of local convention, and cannot claim any universal validity.

scepticism   Doubt about whether any knowledge is possible, either at all or in a particular context.

science   The pursuit of knowledge by empirical means, through observation and experiment.

scientific progress   The process whereby science cumulatively brings us greater knowledge and understanding, so that changes in scientific beliefs are not arbitrary.

scientism   The belief that modern science, with its empirical methods, exclusively determines what is true.

secularism   The determination to describe and explain everything without appeal to religion.

self   Whatever 'I' am – the subject of rationality, and not necessarily to be identified with the body. Its existence is much contested, as being too metaphysical.

sense–data   The foundations of our knowledge, as understood by empiricist philosophers – traditionally seen as 'raw' and uninterpreted, though part of our conscious experience.

sociobiology   The biological study of the evolution of social behaviour in all organisms, including humans (similar to so-called evolutionary psychology).

soul   The part of the human person which allegedly survives death.

spirit   A vague term that sometimes seems merely to mean what is not material. Used in a more positive sense it refers to a higher level of reality than the physical.

supernatural   Whatever lies in principle beyond the natural world, and the scope of physical science.

supervenience   The idea that one set of properties somehow depends on another set without being reducible to them.

teleological   Associated with purpose, rather than being the mere product of arbitrary causes.

theism   The traditional belief in a God who is related to this world and can intervene in it, whilst still being separate from it.

theology   The systematic study of the nature of God.

tradition   The inherited understanding from previous generations, taking many forms, including the institutions, general presuppositions and prejudices, passed on to us.

transcendental argument   The appeal to the necessary conditions, and presuppositions, for the occurrence of a practice, such as science.

truth   Often seen as a property of language, when it reflects the way things actually are (or 'reality'). The relativist may see truth rather as a product of social agreement. 'Truth' is a central notion in philosophy, and its nature has been much contested.

universe   The totality of what exists physically in space and time, at least in theoretical interaction with us. Alternative universes would by definition be removed from any possible contact with our world.

verification   The checking by experience of claims to truth.

verification principle   The principle that only what can be publicly checked can be accepted as meaningful.

Index

Printed in the United States
127797LV00004B/4/P